Psalm

/sä(l)m/

"to pluck"
("the twanging of a harp.")

A sacred song from the heart;
spiritual aspiration of the soul;
a song of praise to God

Psalms

LIFE
IS A

PSALM

DaJuan Bell

Life Is a Psalm
A Seasonal Expression for the Times in Life

Copyright 2023 © DaJuan Bell

For inquiry or wholesale, please contact DaJuan Bell at byh1sgrace@yahoo.com

ISBN: 979-8-9894166-7-7

Dedication

I'd like to thank my Lord and Savior Jesus Christ for
making life worth living. My life partner Julexa for being
a wife who makes life meaningful. My three children
Asa, Parker, and Bishop for making life exciting.
My sister Sherrie for making life substantial.
My brother Shannon for making life bearable.
My mentor Elder Herbert Parker for making life sensible,
and my late father in the Gospel, Pastor Howard A. Swancy,
for making life achievable.

Dear reader, welcome to my psalm.

Divine intervention through the biblical psalms has inspired me to write a few letters to you. *Life Is a Psalm* will give you a curious and raw take on humanity through my turbulent lens. I desire to take an artful and raw approach to this undertaking to provide a sense of justice for what is possible in God through my eyes. A deep sense of urgency is conveyed in biblical invitations to accomplish all that we are called to do and to overcome great adversity.

This project, for me, is my life, and I'm showcasing it for you to see, experience, and know. If God is perfected in our weakness, He will be strong in this text. The testimony of God in our stories allows us to redeem our past and make way for our future. Let us experience *life as a psalm* in its moments of victory and loss. May God be glorified in our tribulations so our life can be a seed for others.

I pray that you will be blessed in reading and hearing these words.

The Shadow
That Shapes Me

Convoluted but true, my thoughts at the ripe old age of twelve began to shift toward death. My external reality was pushing on my mind and my world, and it was changing so fast that I couldn't keep up with my thoughts. My mother asked me, "Would you like me to die here or in the hospital?" As if that's a decision a twelve-year-old needs to make for their dying mother. The burden of choice and the burden of the unknown are greater than many can comprehend. Of course, the question in itself was irrelevant. However, it opened the door to the next seat of my life, and everything in my life was about to change.

What was a young boy to do after losing his mother, best friend, guide, and the only authority in his life while falling into the abyss? A physical and emotional abyss. Perhaps I died that day with her, and the life I continued to live was hell to me. My childhood and innocence vanished with her passing. I became a robot in this messed-up world without any structure, guide, or teacher. Survival was my new parent and friend. It taught me to steal for food. Imagine a hunger so great that even eating doesn't fulfill its demands. I would sleep wherever I could, in a car, on a park bench, or on someone's floor. Making it through to the next day was often my only goal.

A sense of structure was appealing to me because I had nothing. When you're left with nothing, you'll cling to anything. This was my introduction to street life and criminal underworld gangbanging in Los Angeles, which would become my reality. Barbaric was the assignment. Every day I would find myself at the depths of a deep dark pit, facing harm or under the constant threat of violence.

Death was hunting my mind, will, emotions, and physical body every day. I once had a death sentence pronounced over me by a street jurisdiction judge and was announced guilty by a street jury. Even in hell, there's a structure and order for how the chaos should run.

Fear and uncertainty became my familiar friends. I often had conversations with death and the idea of God, trying to reason with my situation and life. *What's the point of all this? Is there anything more significant outside of my reality?* Sometimes I would mumble prayers, aimless prayers, of hope and desperation for things to change. I didn't know who I was talking to. Something started stirring inside of me, though, knowing that I wanted more out of life than to mistreat myself and others around me. I thought, *Perhaps there's something better.*

A woman came onto the scene, and she became like a mother to me. She appeared at a critical moment in my life and sparked my curiosity amid my chaos. I could see how different things were for her. I could see the way that she dressed and the way that she talked and carried herself. She spoke about herself with a sense of value and purpose. She listened to different music that wasn't filled with hatred. Her choice of words was different than mine. I couldn't shake the idea that she was different. I needed to know why and how. She became my mentor and showed me the light.

A course was set for my transformation as I would learn and grow from one mentor to the next. My invitation to learn more about myself and God became evident daily. This elevated my lifestyle to something sustainable, where

I could become a husband, father, and family leader. My transformation was simply starting, and I didn't know that a few years of hell would take my entire life to unravel. I could see both trees in the garden for the first time in my life.

Sometimes the darkest days paint the opportunity for great light to be shown. Each of us, with our unique stories and callings, can highlight and make a redemptive use of our darkest hours. Our meaning and purpose are often found in how we respond to our situations in life.

Rather than seek perfection in our lives, let us seek Him as we often stumble on the path of life. He will be strong where we might fail ourselves and those around us. Our lives will turn into a psalm of praise because He is Great and Mighty. Let us look at humanity's facets, splendor, and pain to embrace, understand, and grow. This is my letter to you. I pray that it will lead you and guide you in every season of life.

Invitation Into Seasonality

It's easy to embrace life's fantastic realities and ignore everything else. It might not be ignorance; it might be selective attention. It just doesn't feel good to talk about the other stuff. It might be helpful, but it doesn't make us comfortable. Interestingly enough, the life that we were brought into has challenging juxtapositions built within it on either side. Seldom is a child born into this world without the mother feeling tremendous pain and stretching.

As she stares into her newborn's eyes, does she not feel the pain from the process while experiencing new life simultaneously? Is that not life? Who entered the world without this process?

The pain in childbirth is attributed to decisions that were made in the garden. In essence, we're taught that the idea of Good and Evil is our current reality because sin has introduced itself into our lives. So, there's no escaping this human process of good versus evil. Everyone comes in and goes out the same way. We don't have it any other way.

In addition to our lives being built upon the ebbs and flows of sin and grace, we also embrace the seasonality of life.

Within each decade of one's life, there is a seasonal expression. Sometimes the seasons happen to us; sometimes, we dictate their origin based on our decisions. The art of life is knowing what season you are in so you can partner with it and not fight it. Some seasons are pleasant, and some seasons are rather unpleasant. In some seasons, we can control and embrace the journey and the outcome, while in others, we have no control. This is life. It would be nice if life was always butterflies and rainbows, but it is not.

This tension is far too common and relatable to everyone. So relatable that it's hard to understand and embrace.

Why would I want to embrace such a balanced take on humanity when it would be so much nicer to just talk about the positives? It's because we can't escape ourselves. We can't escape our need to purge bad things from us. Sometimes we need to weep for the things that hurt us. Sometimes we need to heal from the trauma of our past. Sometimes we must die daily, just as the Apostle Paul asks us to.

But why? What is the point of enduring the cognitive process of the tension of life if not to find ourselves in it, to find our purpose and our meaning, to find a reason to live, to find reasons to love? We're not living until we find out why. Also, as we explore the process of humanity and its ups and downs and embrace every season of life that comes our way, we will find Him in it. He will be there when we find ourselves in seasons of thriving and loss and in times of harvest and drought, He will be there. Every season under the sun is not new to Him as it might be to us. We will see the creative genius in Redemption and enjoy the partnership that we have created.

Eternal
Considerations

In everything, we shall have prayerful supplication. Is not everything we do tied to some Eternal purpose? Not only the consideration of one's life but the reality in which we live by a Divine utterance. It's easy to see God in everything if we open our eyes for just a moment. Are we so into ourselves that we're unaware of the Divine in the midst of our day?

Some may say that the absence of some emotion or lack of some overarching restrictive nature to prevent evil means that God is not always among us. How could that be? Has He not given us the creative freedom to become the very thing we desire? Do we not have the capability to produce our own realities single-handedly? Is not the nature of our existence alone the handy work of the Father?

In everything we do, we must do so with eternal consideration. This does not negate the raw and hard-to-digest parts of ourselves that bring us to honest conversations and honest conclusions about the areas that we have a great need in and the areas of great victory. Biblically-based conversations encompass every part of humanity. Is not the process of David in the psalms speaking of the very nature of Jesus even through his deep trials and tribulations? Is God not exalted in every facet of who we are because some believe He's only interested in the polished versions of our perfected nature?

The Bible clearly states that God accepts everything we have to bring. We are not set up simply to arrive at a destination; we are positioned for a relationship. A relationship with Him, with ourselves, and with those around us. Are we somehow bound from receiving our heavenly inheritance today? Is Heaven not comprised of peace, joy, and righteousness? Some would have you believe that Heaven is for tomorrow, but Christ would invite you to see that it is actually for today.

Self-Reflections

Our life is an epistle built on the backdrop of our response to eternal considerations. What will we do with the life that we're given? How will we choose to respond in times of plenty and in times of drought? What choices will we make that determine what kind of person we will become? That is the purpose of this book: that we may find Opportunities in our own stories and in His to discover meaning and strength.

We shall find ourselves and discover ourselves while we're on life's journey. We should arrive at some understanding of our Maker not by the situation and circumstances we experience but by the revelation of His grace in the midst of those. Self-reflection has its purpose and meaning if we realize who we are a reflection of. How will we change if we enter into self-reflection and only see ourselves? We don't simply live for ourselves, nor did we decide by ourselves to initiate this thing called life. We are not our own; we are His. He did not simply die for us, but He died as us; therefore, we are alive in Him.

Let us continue our life as a psalm and not ignore any facet that may come our way. We will be reborn in the renewing of our minds with the Eternal consideration of our past. Knowing deep down inside that our lives have intrinsic value and importance, and we don't know the breadth and depth of our temporal experience. We cannot see through time to see when it will end. Therefore, our relationship with time should be understood, feared, and humbly sought after. Time has its own mind; it continues at the pace that it wills, and we cannot change that. We can't plead and convince time to slow down or speed up based on our desires. So, we must embrace the reality that there's a time for everything and live our life on time.

Psalms

This is the beginning of the psalms on time.
I pray that you will glean and grow in the urgency
of understanding the season of life you're in and how
you can invite God into it. We all embark on a sacred song,
a hymn of praise, sometimes with tears and sometimes
with laughter. He is delighted with it all.
Let us remain diligent in pursuing grace
as we interact with time.

Time to Kill

There's Time to Kill. The choice is ours. Does not the Bible say that the power of life and death is within us? Of course, we have a devil who comes to steal, kill, and destroy. Is he alone the only one who has the capability to kill? People might wonder, how could you say such a thing? It's naive to assume that we don't have the capability to kill ourselves, and therefore, we're allowing things that should be dead to live on and destroy us from within. It is a Biblical concept to allow grace to run out in an area of our lives so that we may transition into New Life. Does not Jesus propose such a thing? Does He not ask us to die with Him so that we may be raised with Him? Shouldn't our thoughts that exalt other gods be put to rest so that He may live in our mind? Why would we give the devil so much credit if we hang on to things that destroy us?

Yes, as Christians, we should entertain A Time to Kill. I'm not talking about bodily harm and breaking up the most sacred Commandments. I'm talking about putting to bed our former selves and taking up the Commandment of the Apostle Paul as he proposed that we die daily to ourselves so that His grace can renew us. This self-killing is the most humble thing we could do to renew ourselves with God every day, rather than trying to live on our own ideals with our own power in the hell that we've developed and inherited.

Every day, I lived in hell as a gang member; I don't want that former self to live within me now. I must put to work the power that I've been bestowed from on high to kill off the former self that brought me death and destruction to position myself for Resurrection in him. My past is not eliminated. My past is still very present. The difference is it's washed in blood. Not blood from my hands in the wielding of my sword but the blood from the cross that has the power to redeem me.

See, even Christ used death strategically to advance freedom. Most beautifully, he could leverage the proper time to kill without harming anyone. Christianity and the salvation offered through Jesus would not be possible if He didn't offer Himself up as the Living Sacrifice. Sacrifices also take the life of something holy and pure for the greater good. We sacrifice daily for ourselves and others just as Christ sacrificed Himself for us.

Do we wield such a power to bring death to certain things for us to see life? Is not Jesus in charge of life and death? Who do you think gave the devil his power? Perplexing, yes; confusing, yes; interesting, yes. Nevertheless, the Bible calls us "little gods." We entertain this power. We can speak life and death over anyone or anything at any time. We can exalt belief systems in our life and kill them the next moment. We can birth a dream in one second and kill it the next.

The spiritual world is built around the same principle that we see in the physical world. Can we not physically bring life and death by our own hands? Of course, we can. We do it every day. The difference is the power of life and death needs to be used strategically and in correlation with our relationship with Christ and humanity. Because even though we have this power of life and death, we should not wander around with our sword swinging needlessly at anything that walks by us lest we harm someone. We should be strategic to eliminate those things that keep us from life, liberty, and our God-given personal freedoms while simultaneously feeling the bit in our mouth to restrain us from needless pain.

Read, Pray, Reflect

"I will freely sacrifice unto thee:
I will praise thy name, O LORD; for it is good."

PSALM 54:6 KJV

Sacrifice requires something to die, what are you willing to kill in order to live your divine purpose?

_____

_____

_____

_____

_____

_____

_____

_____

_____

_____

_____

_____

_____

_____

_____

_____

_____

Time for Birth

There's always a time to be born. Of course, in the flesh we're born once, but those who are born of the spirit are born again. This renewal is an invitation from God to renew the parts of us that continue beyond our current state into an everlasting one. God is calling us into this renewal by using our language. He said that just as you were born into this world, you will need to be born again by the spirit of life, the Holy Spirit. This birth takes place through a combination of acceptance, understanding, revelation, and continued belief.

It's hard to cognitively digest the idea that if we believe in something, it will become our reality. Still, if we use the same understanding that Christ gave us, which is to correlate our humanity with the spiritual world, we see how we create our realities daily. Our belief systems generate the activity that happens in our lives and therefore dictate our outcomes. Faith is actually very practical. If I look at my neighbor and desire good things from our relationship, I will work hard to make that happen. If I look at my neighbor and desire bad things out of our relationship, I will work hard to make that happen. Our minds operate as a self-fulfilling prophecy continuously.

This is why we must be born again in our spirit, soul, and mind. The language and the correlation of Christ's process speaks of new beginnings. We are starting over, and we're moving on from our past. First, we have to understand Christ's death for this to be possible, and then we are able to incorporate new life. This new life is essential for us to accept change and the possible realities available in Christ. It's not just a symbolic acceptance. We are actually becoming someone different than before. The Bible refers to us as a New Creation, something never seen on Earth or in Heaven.

The conclusion of the garden was the embodiment of man entertaining good versus evil instead of an exclusive Divine relationship with God. When we accept a new birth from God, we accept this Divine relationship while we are in the midst of a life filled with Good and Evil. It is as crazy and awesome as it sounds. Before, Adam and Eve had a choice between the two and were kept from the Divine relationship because it would have helped them in that Eternal state of sin. Now, we are invited into this Divine relationship as we continue to overcome the knowledge of Good and Evil.

Is not every thought birthed into our existence at some point? Do we not give offspring to those positive and negative thoughts in our minds? It's an invitation to analyze our belief systems and perceptions to differentiate between reality and fiction and our accepted belief systems. We give birth to new ideals every day. My life began to change and transform when my mentors helped me exchange one belief system for another, one thought for another. I became a new person because what I believed about myself was born again. I would birth new thoughts that provided me with life instead of death. This process was miraculous yet very practical. All my prayers and insistence for change drove me to inquire and align myself for something greater.

There's almost always a time for birth. The realization we must have is to continually give birth to the things that God wants us to be mindful of and incorporate. An analogy for the process of birth is that a seed is planted after a time of preparation into fertile soil, where incubation and nurturing occur to ensure that that seed can come to life. The same process happens to us. I use the word "process" because it's most definitely a process. Many out there desire great and meaningful change without a process. This isn't the case, though, in birthing something new. It takes time, nurturing, and a committed process.

The correlation between birth and miracles is an interesting one. We know that birthing something takes significant time and resources, but wouldn't we say the same thing about miracles? When a mom is giving birth to her child, doesn't the child come into existence at a moment's notice? The same thing happens with miracles. They come from a fully immersed and developed place, ready to be birthed immediately. The same thing happens with our thoughts and our beliefs. We embody them until they're good and healthy so we can birth them into the world. The gift of self-control allows us to restrain birthing these thoughts to the wrong people or prematurely. We want the things we've been cultivating in our hearts, spirits, and minds to live beyond us just as Jesus's thoughts live beyond Him.

When in doubt, embrace the unknown journey of Christ so that we may be renewed and born again in every way. No one else can offer this to us. No education, no other God, not even self-reasoning and intellect. This is a holistic transformation we are very much a part of. The birth that we incorporate into the world can live outside us for a very long time in ways we cannot imagine. What are you birthing today?

Read, Pray, Reflect

"They will come and declare his righteousness; to a people yet to be born they will declare what he has done."

PSALMS 22:31 CSB

Has God impregnated you with a vision?

Why haven't you given birth to it?

_____

_____

_____

_____

_____

_____

_____

_____

_____

_____

_____

_____

_____

_____

_____

_____

_____

_____

_____

_____

_____

_____

_____

_____

_____

_____

_____

Read, Pray, Reflect

Time to Weep

To weep is to purge our system with some emotional release. Interestingly, tears represent an external, visual washing. I'm sure there are scientific reasons why we cry to process something with our thoughts or our emotions. Why do we weep if it's not for some symbolic shedding? Visually speaking, the eyes are the window to the soul, and when we cry, we cleanse our soul.

Weeping is housed under the umbrella of our emotional state. The trauma we've experienced in life speaks directly to how we carry ourselves emotionally. Are we short-tempered, numb, emotionless? Do we bury our emotions to never see them again? Did our culture or upbringing train us not to exhibit emotions because emotions show weakness?

Traditionally, women are more prone to being aware of their emotions and having emotional experiences than men are. If you consistently deny yourself from having an emotional experience, then you are training your mind, body, and soul that you do not value these messengers. Sometimes, we are experiencing so much pain and trauma that we have to turn off our emotions altogether because we are in survival mode. In this case, it might be hard to cry and weep because we deny ourselves the ability to feel pain.

We've convinced ourselves that if we feel pain, we must process and make sense of it. This is a tall order, and sometimes our traumas are incomprehensible. We're afraid to feel because if we feel the level of deep emotional pain that we think we're about ready to experience, we may be broken forever. It's much easier to become numb, insensitive, rigid, and shut out emotions. We could even tell ourselves that crying is for babies or losers who aren't strong enough to keep it together. We'll tell ourselves anything and convince ourselves of anything to not feel that pain again. This kind of pain, though, doesn't go away on its own. There's a time in everyone's life when we must purge our emotions, cleanse our thoughts, and weep.

Jesus wasn't afraid of weeping. The Book of John hosts the shortest scripture in the Bible, yet it's one of the most profound. Jesus, having been out of town, was made aware of Lazarus's death. On the fourth day, He conversed with Mary and Martha, and it seemed everyone else was listening and watching. Now, Jesus knew He was going to raise Lazarus from the grave. He knew that his sleeping was going to be temporary.

Nevertheless, He decided to meet Martha and Mary and everyone watching in their pain, and He wept with them. This made Him remarkably humble and approachable. It could easily be said of Jesus that He didn't actually need to weep because He is an All-knowing God. He wept not only for Himself; He also wept for us.

The fruit of weeping makes us tender, pliable, and humble. It brings us to an understanding of our sensitive lives. The pain, the trauma, and the frailties of life all need to be purged so that they do not destroy us. Every lie deserves a tear, and every misconception and every mistaken identity that we personify needs to be changed and released. Weeping is not simply for extra hydration in our eyes or our cheeks. It is a physical response to an emotional and spiritual reality directly connected to our soul. When we

weep, we align our body, spirit, soul, and emotions.
We align ourselves, and in our prophetic act, we align those around us.

The strongest thing you could do in some situations is to embody and release the experience through weeping. When my mother asked me where she should die, she started to burst into tears, weeping. I matched her emotional pain with weeping. Unknowingly, I was relating to her emotional experience and aligning myself with her pain. Of course, I felt this alone after I understood what she was experiencing. We were brought together at that moment, and my body and my mind only provided me with one outlet for this overwhelming reality I was experiencing. It was to pause and weep.

God designed us in such a way that if we get out of alignment, we have a way to get back on track. If we experience something so incredibly negative that we have no idea what to do with it, we have a way to respond. If our mind can't comprehend and is overwhelmed by the situation in life, we have a way to communicate. If the world is having difficulty processing life's frailties, they have a path of cleansing available. Sometimes, we've neglected this process because it's inconvenient for our emotions. We've convinced ourselves that we don't have time to cry. However, we have no idea how much time we are actually losing because we're misaligned, confused, and numb by our past. There's always a time to weep because it allows us to move forward. It's time for you to reschedule some past neglected appointments.

Read, Pray, Reflect

"For his anger endureth but a moment; in his favour is life:
Weeping may endure for a night, but joy cometh in the morning."

Psalm 30:5 KJV

What are some of the things that bring tears
to your eyes, good or bad?

God uses your tears to water the fruit of your progress,
are you holding back from Him?

_____

_____

_____

_____

_____

_____

_____

_____

_____

_____

_____

_____

_____

_____

_____

_____

_____

_____

_____

_____

_____

Read, Pray, Reflect

Time to
Laugh

God, bring us splendor and bring us laughter! We know you sit in the heavens and laugh at the schemes of man and those who plot against you. Do you bellow and laugh in the innermost parts of yourself in an expression of absurdity so that those around you and those who can hear you realize that you're the Victor? Do you laugh from intense enjoyment and peace? Do you feel satisfaction when your enemies fall around you?

It's almost like laughter is a spiritual echo reverberating through our body and vocal cords. You gave us this echo chamber. We can embody a thought or feeling and then billow out nonsensical speech from the innermost parts of ourselves in the form of High Praise through laughter. How else could you define such an anomaly? You alone, God, sit in the heavens and laugh? Is not the idea of laughter Divine and the utterance the speaking of tongues?

Remember when you surprised Sarah in the beginning of time about her having a child at a later age? You showed up to her with promise and Grace, resulting in a new birth and life. How much of Sarah's laughter and those who laughed around her helped to bring about this promise? It was almost as though she shook off and stretched her old ways in deep, tremendous laughter to prepare for this new life. Is not your sense of humor mesmerizing? Please help me to understand your ways.

Is not laughter a vehicle for joy to be expressed? Does it help us break free from our old ways and invite an unquenchable, incomprehensible Joy? Is that what you did for Sarah? Surely her laughter was to invite in the promise rather than to reject it on the simple basis of her partnering with joy. It was almost as though you simultaneously set up everyone to partake in this joyful expression. You alone can make cities laugh whenever you choose.

My troubled parts want to know if it's time to laugh. Does laughter mean I need to have it together, have all my insecurities sorted and my identity solved? Is laughter my way to get through those difficult times? It's like you instilled within me the mechanisms to transition my moments and transition my seasons with Joy.

"You can laugh and cry, but you can't do both at the same time" was something that Mr. Walker said to me often. Human anatomy has been set up in a way where we're only allowed to do one at a time. On the rarest of occasions, we have tears of joy broken up with laughter. Laughter sends a chemical reaction to the brain to put us in a positive state and tells us that things are okay. We know that you've built this chemical hack into the hard wiring of our bodies to uplift us and bring us to more positive mental and emotional states.

We know you've given us an out whenever we feel down to bring us joy and reset our bodies to a different mood. Perhaps we have the tools, such as laughter, to invite in the promise of what you have for us versus feeling stuck in our feelings for our situations. You made laughter a medicine for us so that we can take it as we need it. How did you know the way to improve our mental state? Oh, it's because you designed us.

I will deploy this medicine for myself and those around me because if you sit in the heavens and laugh, it will be good for me. Now, I have a family, and when my son Parker feels down, I know how to get him to laugh. I tickle him, and I laugh with him, and he can't resist it. Who can resist genuine, joy-filled laughter? Sometimes Parker gets into some trouble by being stubborn and mean. He always snaps out of it when I get him to laugh. It breaks his emotional and cognitive cycle and resets it. Laughter sets us free. Laughter unites us. Laughter provides us with the universal language of positivity and optimism.

Questions still abound, God, about how we implement these Heavenly tools that feel so natural to us that we discount them. Do you not hide things in plain sight for us to find them when we have a revelation of Who You Are? How many people walk the earth today who have no clue of the power you've given them? They're unaware of their divine origin and their divine purpose, and who you are. These things are revealed to us in ways that we cannot comprehend. Maybe we should sit back and have a good laugh.

Read, Pray, Reflect

"We were filled with laughter, and we sang for joy. And the other nations said, "What amazing things the Lord has done for them."

Psalms 126:2 NLT

Think of times when you had a genuine laugh,
what caused this?

Are there areas that you are taking too seriously that
need to be laughed at and let go?

Read, Pray, Reflect

Time to
Heal

The rejuvenation of our bodies and our minds is part of being human. For days, I lay in bed with new stitches from a surgery I had in my thirties. I had my appendix taken out suddenly after being diagnosed with appendicitis.
This was my first major surgery, and I had never experienced anything like this. I was told that if I didn't have the procedure, I might die of some complications. So, I went through the procedure, and now I was lying in the hospital bed with stitches. It's different to consider healing when it comes to your physical body rather than your thoughts or your emotional self. Healing your physical body is so demanding. You can see the way that things should be, but you have a gaping hole and blood coming out of it. It's easy to say that the wound needs to heal. I can't just ignore it lest I die.

My wound needs to be taken care of. I need to give it time and space so that my body can help me repair what once was order and stability. Sometimes, when we're physically, emotionally, and mentally injured, we need to take time to heal. If we ignore our wounds, then we might die inside. If I ignore the wounds of my emotional past, I no longer allow my emotions to live, and they might die.

We should not forsake the time for healing. The Divine process for complete healing takes time. The time needed is based on the trauma. As soon as I got my appendix taken out, I couldn't wait to start walking again, but it took time for my body to regain the strength necessary. When I took my first steps afterward, I felt like I would fall because of the medication and the pain. I tested my healing with help and realized I needed more healing. I needed more time.

If you're alive today, you've been through some emotional, mental, and sometimes physical trauma. There's a time to heal. Did you participate in the time necessary for you to heal from those wounds from long ago? If not, you might need to forgive yourself for not caring enough to take care of your wounds. You might feel ashamed, guilty, and angry for not loving yourself enough to care for those wounds. Perhaps you didn't know how. Perhaps you didn't know that you should. Perhaps they convinced you that this is normal life. Perhaps the pain got you through those moments, and so you've developed a friendship with the pain.

Who says I need to take care of these things? Your traumas are in your speech, written on your face. They dress you every morning and walk you down the street every day. You're only lying to yourself by saying they don't exist. A self-fulfilling prophecy is happening all around you because your traumas affect you. They bleed into your thoughts, emotions, and actions. If they're not taken care of, then they fester, and they create wounds that destroy us inside and out along with our relationships because we live our lives based on our traumas.

You are worthy of getting healing and taking care of yourself. Of course, we know that, not on your own Merit, but on His Merit and accomplishments. God comes to heal our wounds and our afflictions, Sometimes instantly and sometimes through a process. Call on Him; pursue the healing like your life depends on it. Seek life-affirming mental health care and surround yourself with an environment that's conducive to your healing. You can do it!

What could you do if you took time to heal? How much would your life change? Do you have hope for a different future that excludes the pain and traumas from the past? Imagine waking up in the morning and only experiencing and thinking about your present moment and future because you're healed and took time to heal from your past. What's stopping you from healing? No, what's really stopping you from healing? Once you've taken the time and reasoned with yourself, hopefully, you'll find that healing is the only option. Opinions don't fix the wounds of the past. Healing is the only way; maybe it's time for you to heal.

Read, Pray, Reflect

"Have compassion on me, Lord, for I am weak. Heal me, Lord, for my bones are in agony."

PSALMS 6:2 NLT

Have you taken a deep look inside at the things you are hoarding that need healing to know how you can move past them?

Do you believe God is able to heal you?

_____

_____

_____

_____

_____

_____

_____

_____

_____

_____

Time to
Tear Apart
(Rend)

The path to successfully becoming the highest version of yourself will mostly be a lonely road. You'll find that some of the close relationships you've cherished will become strained. Even amongst your family, you might come against much opposition that will try to get you to remain who they've always known you to be. They may persuade you to stay the way you've always been.

There has to be change to become the highest version of yourself. Jim Rohn says nothing changes until you change. With every change, people around us will start to respond and treat us differently, especially if they aren't operating at the same capacity of their potential and living in mediocrity. There's a delicate balance of where we were and where we are now and how people associate with that. Our unchanged surroundings would probably start to dislike our new reflections. It's provoking because they remain unchanged while we renew ourselves.

The subconscious mind is always scanning our environment for unfamiliar circumstances. The subconscious mind is the most powerful machine known to life; it will work to eliminate any threat it detects that takes you away from a state of homeostasis or the state of balance, comfort, and stability. When we change, we affect the status quo of the people around us. This may put us at odds with them. We become an opposing force because we're changing their homeostasis. Our renewal becomes a disruptor for their environment. Now, they must spend time, energy, and emotional regulation in order to adjust to our continued growth. Our growth is not very fun for them because they have autopilot routines.

What is the result of our expansion in life? Sometimes, we break away from those things we knew and those with us. When they see us, they no longer see who we are, but they see a different person. We are different people because we believe differently; therefore, we act differently. Our change makes us unrecognizable from our old selves and ways; therefore, we can't associate with past activities the same way we used to. It's the same reason that Jesus was rejected in His hometown. The people around Jesus were familiar with their past association with who they thought He was and fully rejected Him when He changed their minds. He went from being their friend to their enemy.

A good farmer knows when to plant and when to till. When you till the land, you break it up. This is a natural process to break up what was so that you can prepare for what is to come. It also removes any remnants that might get in the way of future growth. If you never till the land, then your growth will be extremely diminished because of all the excess and the dead foliage. This farming analogy is simple, but we do the same thing. Remember, the Lord shows up with an ax, ready to take down any tree that does not produce fruit. This doesn't sound like fun at all. Sometimes fun is not the goal, but survival is; growth is. To grow, we must allow the ax to be laid upon every dead tree in our lives and break away from those who hold us back, lest we feed off the root systems of the dead relationships.

This process of rending and tearing apart from what once was doesn't need to happen all the time. It's to maintain balance and growth. This pruning is natural in life and is healthy. As much as it is painful, it is fruitful. The pain comes from the emotional attachments and what could be and the grieving of that process. This rending and tearing apart is a symbolic expression of your humanity and returning back to those things that keep you free and unbound in your potential.

Through life, we become bound by things that hold us back. Sometimes, it's our fault; sometimes, we have nothing to do with it. It's easy to be in the middle of something and feel like our only option is to remain and dwell on our lack of freedom and life. But we have a higher calling than just simply to remain. We are called to thrive in life, which sometimes takes great Sacrifice by letting go of things we once knew. Breaking Free and breaking away is difficult, but if we value our life the way we should, it's the only path forward. It's time to tear apart those things that hold us back.

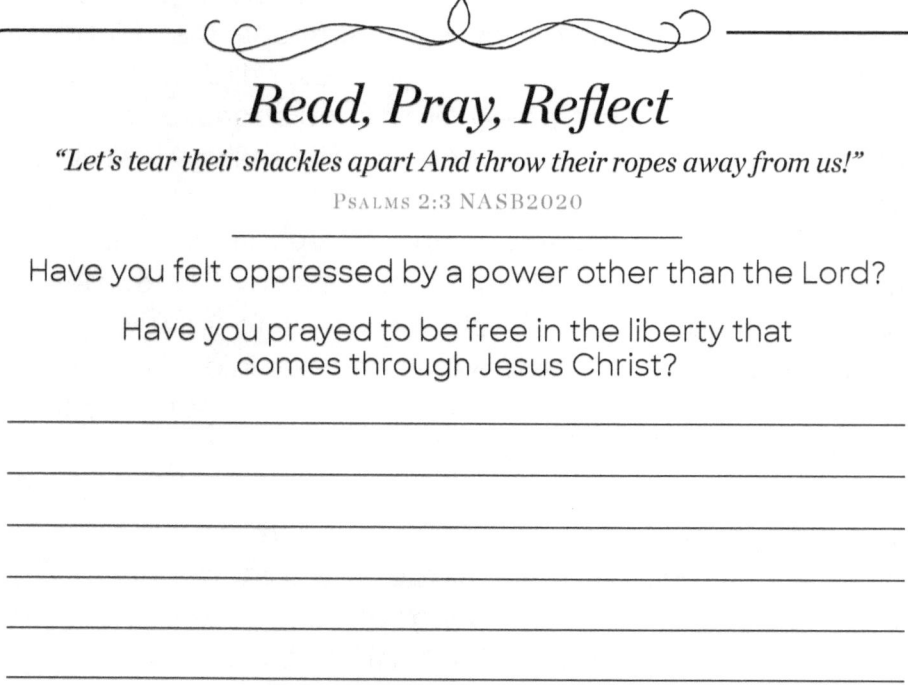

Read, Pray, Reflect

"Let's tear their shackles apart And throw their ropes away from us!"
Psalms 2:3 NASB2020

Have you felt oppressed by a power other than the Lord?

Have you prayed to be free in the liberty that comes through Jesus Christ?

_____

_____

_____

_____

_____

_____

_____

Time to Build Up

There are times when God gives us nails instead of a sword. He gives us a hammer instead of a pillow. This was the case for Noah and even Jesus. They were called to be carpenters because they were builders. Imagine all of the professions that they could have picked up instead. Carpentry was the number one option for a reason. They weren't called to be fighters or called to a season of rest. It was time to build something.

See, God seeks out a willing carpenter when the world needs a vessel. He doesn't need perfection; He needs someone who can apply themselves and create with what they're given. Builders are visionaries with practical skills. Not too much different from you and me. They're no more special than us. The difference in what they do is they take something theoretical and build it practically One Nail at a time. Oh, the desire to have the established House of peace and prosperity that we all want. But do we have to put the work into it first? Nobody wants to do that. We'd all prefer that it be built for us so we can claim it as our own.

Aren't we called to the promised land filled with milk and honey? The city that we desire to dwell in is empty. It's but a desert parking lot with rocks and sand. What are we to do? Shall we return to Egypt because they had temporary dwellings for us? Or shall we find the blueprints of Our Lives and pick up the nails needed to build something suitable? Perhaps a vessel that our family can dwell in? Perhaps God will help us build it as He is well acquainted with our needs.

Where oh where do we find the materials needed? If God has called us to build such a thing, shall He not provide the necessary materials? Was Jesus left unequipped to complete the work necessary? Surely, God provided Noah with every piece of wood required for the ark. Of course, He did. Those who cast the vision have also been given the provision. If not, then Noah would still be looking for scraps to finish his boat, and every vision would be suspended. God is sure and true.

In certain seasons of life, we are called to build a new vessel to accompany us from one season to the next. If we refuse to participate in building this new vessel, then we stay stuck in our old Shell. We wonder why we can't grow. We wonder why God would keep us here. We take those nails that He gave us and use them to prop up the thing that is falling apart instead of using them to build a new thing.

Building anything starts with a desire and a vision. When I started building my life, I wanted to please the Lord and share the good He had blessed me with. This was tangible to me. I could see it, feel it, taste it. I've built out a Ministry with 2,000 members because of God's vision in my heart. I knew I needed to build something that would accommodate others beyond myself, so I worked continuously to build this thing.

Builders have lasting impact, like the Apostle Paul, who penned a very large percentage of the New Testament. He was a self-professed master craftsman. I don't doubt it. He could take an idea and design its elements down to the minute details, and then, with perfect execution, he could place each variable in its right spot. This is not only a tangible exercise but a spiritual one. We build our worlds and realms in our minds every single day.

There's no limit to our sanctified imagination. No one but ourselves can keep us from building a new world we want to walk into. It is God alone who has given us this ability and skill set. Did He not stand before the earth when it was formless and void and build everything we have today? How much intentionality goes into a perfect plan? Or shall we whimper on the sidelines, complaining about our season and growth?

What will we do with the nails that God placed in our hands? We know what He did with His. He built something so great and so magnificent it saved the world.

Read, Pray, Reflect

"Unless the Lord builds the house, those who build it labor in vain. Unless the Lord watches over the city, the watchman stays awake in vain."

PSALMS 6:2 NLT

What have you built for God?

Are you willing to do the work that The Lord has called you to in order to build yourself into something beautiful for The Kingdom?

_____

_____

_____

_____

_____

_____

_____

_____

Time to
Break Down

Running into life without an internal compass is a recipe for getting lost. We're never short of opportunities. What we're short of is evaluating the right things to devote our attention, time, energy, and resources to. This is a critical process of us breaking down what's necessary in the season of life that we're in and deploying a level of contemplative consideration. This consideration is not foolish but necessary. Only babies, who lack the cognitive function of evaluating and creating a hierarchy of needs, choose what's in front of them.

In a time of no consideration, we are like babies accepting every situation at face value and not prioritizing our needs based on God's design. Are we so fickle to be passive in our life? Shall we have no say in the prioritization of our minds and our actions? Religions across the world blindly accept the outcome as their God. This is extremely detrimental because it means every outcome has become their God. Their participation doesn't have any weight or value. Are we simply waves that should be passed back and forth for eternity? I presume so if we're hopeless and without value.

How are we to challenge the outcome of a scenario? Who are we to inquire upon God? The basis of those questions resides in the fact that you are either in a relationship with God or you are not. A person who is in an active relationship with God asks and inquires about their life in a contemplative and considerate manner. They ask not to challenge but to know. Perhaps this knowledge allows them to challenge, fight, and contend for something greater. A person without a relationship either blankly accepts every scenario as karma in which he worships or blames God for everything that is perceived to be a violation of his own interests. Which person are you?

Providing a means for you to break down your thoughts and your day gives a place for contemplative evaluation. The Bible asks that we consider a matter. Contemplation is not always self-evaluation. Contemplation is immersion that leads to a hierarchy of understanding. This critical thinking provides a means for us to prioritize what's important and then deprioritize what's not. Where do you spend your time? What is the extent of the time you spend on something versus its return in your life? Are you lost in mindless entertainment throughout the day? Do you consume meaninglessness through eight-second video clips online?

Oh, but my pastor said not to judge. The Bible is built on a relationship that always provides two options: don't judge lest you be judged, and judge all things. Why would we have these juxtapositions before us? It's a skill set to apply wisdom in our lives. We're not robots that blanketly accept outcomes. If we want to see change, we must become it. How can one not say that Jesus embodies the word more than the rest of us? Confusion abounds in the actions of Jesus, but if we realize His actions embodied the very word of God, then we know every situation was within His control. Nothing happened to Him. He happened in every situation.

I guess it's the result of bringing your own presence into a room rather than being affected by it. Are we not all thermometers checking the temperature throughout the day? Some of us have thermostats that actually change the temperature of our environment. Which one are you? Have you not considered things you focus on and magnify in your mind? Why were the children of God always requested to look up during a monumental transition? Was there something special in the sky? In most cases, there was nothing special in the sky. They were changing their perspective in their mind. When we change our perspective, we change the elevation in which we see our circumstances. Why else would God have us go to the mountaintops to meet Him? Was there something special in the physical elevation? No. He was helping us create a hierarchy of understanding.

When we talk to God and prioritize the righteous and holy things, we gain an elevated perspective versus the things below. Some of us needlessly accept the voice from the pit; thus, we stay there. We've perfected the art of self-prophecy. The thing we see is the thing we become. This is why we are to remove the pictures of our former selves from the walls of our house lest we become the thing that we were. Shall we not just look up and look upon Him? Lest we fix our eyes on something lesser and idolize the thing that's before us. What is the extent of our gaze worship versus observation?

Shall we not consider a matter as a part of our daily cognitive function? What extent of time do you spend in thought worship versus displaying curiosity? Is it all an internal matter or a spiritual one? Answering these questions will lead us into a relational heaven or a pit of misery, depending on who we serve. Why would God give you a brain If you're not supposed to use it? Do you not have the Holy Spirit within you who assists all of us in this hierarchy of needs? Maybe it's time we break down a matter and consider it before ourselves and before God.

Read, Pray, Reflect

"You have broken down all his walls;
You have brought his strongholds to ruin."

PSALMS 89:40 NASB2020

If you were to contemplate areas in your life
where you struggle in achieving God's plan, what do
you find that you can break down and either remove or
prioritize to make immediate progress?

Are you willing to allow Jesus to break down
the walls you setup in order for you to feel
the full expression of His love?

Read, Pray, Reflect

Time to
Cast Away

When you're in a time of plenty, it's easy to not plan for the future. One would have to consider within themselves the things necessary to sustain life beyond this time of plenty. Planning ahead requires consideration and execution. This is when we're called to cast away or render a portion for another time. It's not simply a savings but a strategic positioning of our resources and time. Imagine the simple fisherman who puts bait on the end of his hook. He's deploying a specific portion of his resources for a future return.

This example extends into the very practical parts of our society with the sowing and harvesting of crops. If the farmer decides to forego the time of casting away the seed, then what crops will he be able to provide next season? The answer is easy. Who could expect a return from nothing invested? No reasonable man or woman could. Within our time of harvest, we should do as the Old Testament says and set apart a portion that's not to be used by us. It's to be used by those who walk by and those who have great need.

The preservation of part of our harvest for the sake of relational gain seems silly, but it's not. The casting away of part of our seed pertains to every area of life. We're not just setting aside part of our income for savings or investing; we are partitioning within each season a percentage of our consumable inheritance of time, resources, energy, and everything else that's measurable. The intentional preservation positions us for our future seasons with food to eat, money stored away, and relational seeds invested. This approach gets us through each season's ups and downs.

Let me tell you a story about Joseph. He was a man after God's heart who ended up in Egypt because of the dream that he shared with his brothers. After he shared the dream with them, they became mad and planned his execution. One of the brothers didn't want to kill him, so they threw him in a pit instead, where he was found by someone else and sold off into slavery. He faithfully worked his way up the ranks and found himself in a desirable position where another woman was advancing upon him, and he denied her requests. This sent him into another pit, but it was a prison this time. Until this point, the only thing that was going for Joseph was the family he was born into, which disavowed him and his dream. Those two things were the extent of what Joseph could bring into this situation.

So, in a predictable God-given fashion, two people around Joseph in prison had dreams, and they looked to him as the Interpreter of these dreams. Joseph could have restrained himself and stayed in pity rather than extend his portion to the two people in need before him. Thankfully, he decided to cast away unto them an interpretation of both dreams. Because what else was he to give in this Moment besides the one thing he had?

Now, let's fast forward in the story. ne of the two gentlemen who had their dreams interpreted by Joseph in prison was later released and was brought before Pharaoh. They remembered Joseph and told Pharaoh about his gift. Being self-absorbed and interested in his dream interpretation, Pharaoh brought Joseph out of the pit. Again, Joseph could have restrained himself in pity and not extended his portion unto Pharaoh. Nevertheless, Joseph extended himself by giving an interpretation of

Pharaoh's dreams. Mind you, Joseph had nothing else to give at this point. He was giving all that he had to sow into his future seasons.

The interpretation was so great that Joseph was placed in charge of Pharaoh's house and land for the next several years. Joseph was to deploy a savings and future investment strategy on behalf of Pharaoh's government to make them tremendously wealthy and save everyone in the land. Also, this saving strategy was to be so successful that Joseph's family would hear about it, and they would be indebted to Joseph in a foreign land.

Joseph could have reserved himself during the times of casting away his seed by communicating his gift. But he did not restrain himself. He gave into his future in every opportunity that presented itself. He planted enough seeds using his gift to make him the number two most important person in all of Egypt, and this power not only saved the country but brought forth a sequence that reconciled him with his family. He saved them and preserved his inheritance in a land called Goshen for a set time. The simplicity with which Joseph acted within his gift can be overlooked, but he was not shy to use his deployable seed to advance him into his future.

The very act of saving and investing to preserve a country is what most people focus on because it's tangible and because we understand the function. But in all things, we should Cast Away our seed for another time. When we talk to others and grow our relationships, shall we restrain our seed? Shall we restrain our seed entirely for ourselves when we share our time or consume our resources?

The answer should always be no. There is a set of spiritual laws that we must abide by.

The casting away of our seed for future seasons is a spiritual law. The idea of procreation is within this law. Our inheritance is not simply for us but for the future. Joseph understood this idea very well, and therefore, he was in charge of everyone. If we can wrap our minds around this, it will unlock our relationships, friendships, personal lives, and future prosperity. Within our time, there's the time to eat, a time of plenty, and a time for harvest, but we should always remember the time to cast away for the next season lest we not have one.

Read, Pray, Reflect

*"Cast your burden on the Lord, and he will sustain you;
he will never permit the righteous to be moved."*

PSALM 55:22 ESV

What do you already possess that you are willing
to cast away as a dedication unto the Lord?

Are you making proper investments
in the important areas of your life?

Time to
Gather Stones
Together

As we wander through life, we find high water marks that indicate moments of memory and reflection. Moments of seasonal marking. In these places, we should often contemplate what we've accomplished and what God has done through us. This was the case for Israel as it is for us today. How could one transpire through life and not look back at the stones of remembrance? Why do you think tombstones are so significant? They help us remember.

When we place our head on the rock, we lean our understanding on something different from our feeble mind. As we look back, we see the interventions of God in the night as one would lay their head on a rock and drift off to sleep. The rock doesn't seem to be the softest pillow, but it's a firm foundation for encounters and remembrances.

Who would we be if we did not gather the stones? Mind you, everyone collects the stones for the most important moments of their life, like their wedding and the funeral. Why would we not do this when we are alive? We gather the stones for legacy and for inheritance. It helps us remember what we've been through, what God has done for us, and where we should go. When we walk through the valley that has troubled us in the past, we can look to our left and to our right and see the pyramid of stones.

This cornerstone is Jesus, positioned well throughout the journey of our lives. When we are in a moment of victory or temptation, the cornerstone is the plumb line that brings us to the proper understanding. What has God done for our ancestors, and what has He done for us? Is He not a miracle worker in our lives? Yes, we find ourselves in autonomous wandering, yet there He is always before us, pointing the way.

Should I cringe when I don't feel empowered? It's easy to wallow in self-pity when the Mundane presses in. Even if God has positioned us to be like John the Baptist and sit in the dirt and eat bitter locusts, we should feel empowered even more so if we are positioned after John the Baptist. Was he not an embodied representation of the old covenant? Even so, he still brought about the remembrance of the former things to usher in what was yet to be.

John, all by himself, baptizing people, repeating himself continuously, could easily get bored, wondering what might happen if he just stopped everything. He couldn't, though; the former things compelled him. He remembered those who came before him, and they painted a picture of who was yet to come. Those stones were piled up on either side of the baptism or remembrance stones, shaped like a cross. With each person, he would dunk them in the water and wonder what might happen. He knew the baptism might be good for them, but he also knew he was one person away from finding the Messiah.

One day, he looked up and saw Jesus on top of the hill, like a great, high mountain, and He was like honey from the rock. John looked up, and his reward was above. There He was, the cornerstone on which everything was built. Imagine looking at yesterday today and forever walking toward you! It would be time to lie down and die in awe-inspiring beauty. He knew he was not worthy of tying his sandals. He brought about a different era. Therefore, as he professed to go away so that Christ could accomplish all He intended, John knew he was a part of Christ's foundation. This gave him meaning and purpose.

We have to see the seasonality of his life and bring it into context with his diminishing effect. John needed to go away so that Christ could dwell here on Earth. You, however, are not John. We are positioned after Christ, so it would be improper for us to try to diminish our effect for some artificial sense of martyrdom.

Do you not see the purpose of David picking up five stones before his great battle with Goliath? Perhaps he needed extra ammo, just in case he missed a few times? This is not at all the case. There were, in fact, five giants that David was supposed to kill. He knew he needed one stone for each giant. Boom! Stones give us perspective! Remembrance stones give us context. Stones give us a vision to see what God has done and what He intends to do. Grab your stones from the brook and prepare to walk into a season of life that only God has prepared for you.

Read, Pray, Reflect

"When the people are gathered together,
And the kingdoms, to serve the LORD."

Psalm 102:22 KJV

God has provided you with resources,
are you using them to your advantage?

_____

_____

_____

_____

_____

_____

_____

_____

_____

_____

_____

_____

_____

_____

_____

_____

_____

_____

_____

_____

_____

_____

_____

Read, Pray, Reflect

Time for
Worship

The contemplation of a person who brings us love and adoration in our hearts and our minds is something we do every day. The profound is often what we measure, but the mundane considerations are the fabric of who we are. Every one of our heart's considerations paints a picture of who we love and desire to be. This is worship! Oh, you thought worship was hands lifted high on Sunday morning at 10:15 after the announcements? Sure, you can worship at that time as well. Worship time is, however, when your heart is turned on with love and adoration. Every electrical charge that flows through your heart the moment it starts beating is an opportunity to worship.

Your body is a testament to worship in the most practical sense. Every breath that you breathe in and out testifies to Yahweh. Breathe in and say the first part of his name. Breathe out and say the second part. The construct of who you are worships Him regardless because it's by design a temple for worship. Did you not know that you're the temple of God? Most of you think the church is the temple in which you go inside to worship Him. When we realize we have the great privilege to worship God in our imperfect state with the Divine tensions of life before us, then we have true worship.

Is worship most impactful when we have it all together or when we're authentic? True worship can be a heartfelt flutter of adoration in the midst of the most difficult seasons. Worship requires a juxtaposition to be present. If no options were given, then our freedom would be compromised. The true Joy in worship is recognizing the option of who to worship. It's not that people don't worship already because they do all the time. The question that remains is who you are worshiping, not whether or not you are worshiping. This is what makes worship so special when it's unto God.

The Bible says He is in our midst. It speaks profoundly that Jesus can be found in our midst just as He is poised on the hill between two others who are being crucified. Even between a thief and a robber, He is found in the moment's tension. Not by Himself as the only option, just as the Garden of Eden presented multiple options. When Adam and Eve ate the fruit, they chose to worship differently than they had done before.

What makes worship different than heartfelt consideration? That is a question for a conscience to decide. Intentionality, however, presents us with more options than not. Our very lives should be filled with the implied intention of exchanging the things we find valuable to us and giving them to God, whether our time, resources, thoughts, actions, or recognition of our Creator. When we create a moment of exchange, this in the very heart of the act is worship. If the exchange doesn't happen, then what kind of worship took place? Oh, sing along, Sally! Karaoke for Jesus! If the heart's not involved, what is?

The words that we express out of our mouths are merely the reflection of our heart's condition. We worship with everything that we focus on and adore. We must be intentional about this lifestyle and exercise extreme caution with whom we worship. This display of value aligns us with the value we express. It is the recognition of who God is and His attributes that bring us to an understanding of these values. In the most unique ways, the more we emphasize an attribute of God, the more we are aware of that very thing. This is why the Bible continuously requests in those appropriate situations to look up and fix your eyes on Him. This fixing our eyes is an attitude of our heart because our eyes are but a mirror to the things we think and believe.

In the moments of intentional worship, miracles tend to happen. Problems seem to disappear. I love worshiping collectively with my home church and can remember one specific time when a young boy who had a brain tumor begged to worship and cry out to God with us. He eventually would make his way back to the doctors, where they reported not being able to locate the tumor anymore! Isn't that incredible? Worship produces miracles; there's always a time to worship. Is this hard for you to believe? If you profess that Christ has the ability to save your soul, but He doesn't have the ability to change someone's body, then you're limiting God and perhaps worshiping the wrong thing. Jesus demonstrated many miracles for the physical body. Is He not the same God He always was, or does our worship limit His expression in our own lives?

Whether you're singing along or in deep contemplation, worship is who you are and who you will be. You are made to worship. The goal in life is to worship the one true God and stay away from false gods and idols that exalt themselves in our hearts and our minds. We are a vessel of praise, and the life that we choose to live is a testament to who we worship. How can you measure a man? It's simple. Find out who he worships. That will tell you more than anything else about him.

Sometimes, it's a time to mourn; other times, it's a time to dance, but I implore you that it's always Time to Worship. Sure, it's important to have designated times of worship, especially corporate worship where you are with others. Exalt His name, giving Him high praise. In addition to those designated worship times, don't neglect every other moment of your life as a sacrifice of praise. We were put here on this Earth as a testament to His goodness, and every thought, every belief, and every action we do is an act of praise to our very creator. It's Always a Time to Worship!

Read, Pray, Reflect

"O come, let us worship and bow down:
Let us kneel before the LORD our maker."

PSALM 95:6 KJV

Have you made Jesus Christ a priority in your life?

What are you doing to show The Lord that
He is worthy of all that you have to give?

Time to Mourn

Part of being human is to know our lives are a gift to us. We were gifted into this world, and our bodies are corruptible. All of creation is corruptible. This provides us with a complex gift. It's a gift because there will be an end, which means there's value in what we have now. If our experience in the flesh lasted forever, then why would it matter? So, transitions are upon us. It's part of the design. We get our turn to live in this moment, as do others. Our maker instilled the exact same emotional compass that He carries. If not, we would not be connected to the people around us.

Does not our blood speak the same language? Are we not made of the same flesh? Did not Christ illuminate every single one of our lives as a flashing light to fertilize the egg that we were created in? Of course, we are interconnected; we are but a string fastened in the tapestry of His design. And if anything should happen in life, whether Great or small, Good or bad, we shall experience it in all of our senses. If a string that is connected to us, in thought, in personal experience, in our blood is broken, then we shall feel that loss down to our bones.

This is part of the human process. If we lose a piece of ourselves, that loss is felt throughout our body and echoes in our minds. The same thing happens if we lose someone around us. I shared with you what took place when I lost my mother. I've even had to experience the loss of friends to senseless violence. What is one to do with the abundance of emotional pain and loss? Shall we carry these feelings and thoughts with us and let them compound over time to never let them out of our shells?

Or shall we embrace a time to mourn and exhibit the most natural emotions in order to express our pain and loss?

One can only carry emotional pain for so long before it starts to fracture oneself. The emotional pain, of course, has a weight to it and a responsibility. It's responsible for expressing itself to anyone who desires to carry it around. It shall be the heaviest yoke that anyone should carry. When we mourn, we participate in a Divine Exchange with our Creator. It takes our yoke and gives us His. This aligns us with the proper process of recalibrating our relationship around gratitude, letting go of the pain, and humbling ourselves so that we may be able to love again.

I'm alive today because I took the time to mourn when I needed to. Let me tell you, I didn't receive a participation award for bringing up my emotional pain in order to confront it. It was difficult because I needed to confront everything I had hoped for that was no longer available. Everything I wish I would have said, I would have known, I would have lived is now different because this individual could no longer participate in my life. My emotions screaming, ready to blame anyone and everyone for my pain. It's natural for us to consider blaming someone else for the reasons we feel instead of confronting the pain for what it is.

There's a reason God put these emotions inside of us. It's so we can develop our own ability to purge realities within us and create new ones. This is exactly what He had to do with us continuously. We meander around in the muck of life and sin before His eyes, and He continually processes the emotional pain of losing His children.

How well do you think He became at mourning us?
I imagine pretty well. Some of us entertain destructive
sin to our souls every single day. No wonder we feel numb
inside; we've tried to kill off our souls. It's time for us to
mourn again and build a new world fully aligned with
Him where we're able to let go of the former things
and people.

Oh, you thought mourning was chasing a feeling away?
No, the process of mourning someone or something
is a spiritual assent. Do you think that you can remove
an emotional reality from yourself and replace it with
one from Heaven? No. Only God can do this for us.
This "natural" gift to heal oneself is only ever possible
with God. Most people get caught up in the idea of sharing
their feelings only to offload the temporary burden of
what they carry inside. This withdrawal is simply ignorance
by trying to expand and dilute the feeling they carry.
Of course, we want to share our feelings, but in sharing,
who can bear such a thing and actually carry it to fruition
but Christ Alone? He's the only one who can carry our
heavy yoke.

Whether we share our feelings with our friends or
with a bottle of alcohol, only God can realign us in this
spiritual assent. Imagine going into a room in Heaven and
having the ability to transfer your emotional pain, loss,
hopelessness, and feelings of separation from those that
you've loved so dearly. This room actually exists inside of
Jesus. Jesus declared before the masses, "In my Father,
there are many places; if it were not so, I would have told
you." Now, you have the right and the access through
Christ alone to exchange your burdens for His reward.

Go on; He will meet you at the exact same spot that you've circled around a thousand times. This time is different, though, because He's with you. He is faithful to meet you there, and if you trust Him, He will be happy to work with you, mend you, heal you from the inside out, and put you back up on your feet. He will provide a defined perspective over time and help you continuously recalibrate your heart so it's pointed in the right direction. Don't mourn alone. He is always waiting.

Read, Pray, Reflect

*"I went about mourning as if for my friend or brother;
I was bowed down with grief, like one mourning for a mother."*

PSALMS 35:14 CSB

What comes to mind when you think about mourning?
Is there perhaps a who that comes to mind?

Are you in a season of mourning?

Have you come out of one not giving yourself
the space to mourn properly?

_____

_____

_____

_____

_____

_____

_____

_____

_____

_____

_____

_____

_____

_____

_____

_____

_____

_____

Time for Harvest

Jesus stared off at a fig tree, hungry and ready to eat. The tree bore big leaves and presented itself as a fruit-bearing tree in season. He lifted up the leaves, and to His surprise, there was no fruit. There must have been quite a conundrum for Jesus because He gave the tree the ability to produce fruit, yet it didn't have any food even though it presented so. Of course, we know the tree was symbolic and physical, but symbolic in the sense that it represented Israel and God was cursing it. It showed the signs of bearing fruit from heaven, but it had no fruit to eat from.

How could God be so harsh on Israel or on the fig tree? Did He not give it the ability to produce fruit and everything required? Is He so demanding that He requires Harvest from a tree that could be out of season? In God's eyes, is there such a thing as being out of season? When we entertain the idea of a harvest, the framework of Ecclesiastes presents itself, where everything has a time and a season.

We must be poised and ready for the opportunity to take in a harvest, whether it's one that we planted or one that was ready for the picking. Jesus was teaching us that a spiritual and eternal harvest is always available. If you are in the right season, then you will be able to access it. God is adamantly against those who present themselves as having a harvest but bear no fruit. The time is now for those who have a harvest and can see a harvest in others.

During my first year I spent in New York, I and my three little children experienced snow for the first time. Seeing the entire ground covered in white, a pure witness I wasn't expecting, was fascinating to me. As I watched my children frolic in the snow and have the time of their lives, I learned about the winter and how devastating it can be if you aren't ready for it. There is a time in which you have to harvest resources that will carry you through because, in times of winter, there isn't anything around for you to harvest. There was so much that I had harvested from my late pastor and mentor, Bishop Swancy. His passing cast a cold spell on a particular area of my life as he was like a father to me. I find myself dealing with my wife and children using those tools he left me with often. I had to harvest when it was time.

One of my biggest regrets is not taking his offer to glean more from him with the time we had remaining together. He was full of wisdom. I was still learning the fundamentals of life at twenty. I did not know that we were living in the time to harvest, and soon that time would end. Can you see the ripe harvest around you, or do you prefer a reactionary life to whatever comes your way? How much of our potential is accessible through seasonality and harvesting when the crop is ready? Did not Jesus wait the perfect amount of time before He started to bear fruit?

The question and assessment for our day is: what aspects are we planting seeds for, and what aspects are we harvesting? In our mind, this may have something to do with time and age. However, God operates off the spiritual realm and time is bypassed. This is why Jesus walked around at twelve years old and baffled the wisest men who lived. Age is subjective. Someone could practice the wrong thing their entire life, which doesn't make them any wiser. However, some people's practice helps them perfect their lives and processes, and it indicates their wisdom.

Every area of life contains a harvest ready to be embraced if you find the right moment and you require the right things from it. Every relationship is set about to birth a harvest that will continue to multiply throughout generations. Imagine how important it is to have children at the right time in your life. If you miss the window of opportunity, then your chances will diminish. This is part of understanding yourself and the time and season you live in. Just like relationships, every single area in our life can bear a harvest. We just need to be open to the idea and then pursue it diligently.

Some people confuse luck with diligence and perseverance. Let me tell you, there's nothing like planting and harvesting something. This is why Jesus spent so much of His time giving us examples of a farmer and his crop. It was as if He continually used us as a metaphor for planting and harvesting throughout the entire Bible. Perhaps that's why He gathered Fishers of Men amongst Himself, so they could be great at collecting and harvesting.

So, how do you know that it's time to harvest? Let's follow the steps of Jesus. First, you feel your heart and your mind with the expectation that there is a harvest because it's designed to be there. Then, you pursue the thing that you desire to gain a harvest from, much like the fig tree. Once you have it dialed in and you can see what you intend to harvest, you check under the leaves to see if there's anything there ready for you. If there's fruit, then it's time to harvest. It seems pretty simple, but for some odd reason, many among us prefer to starve and be a martyr in life rather than collect the harvest around them. Perhaps they feel like they're doing God some type of justice by reducing themselves to nothing. How much more effective would they be in life with God if they were willing to accept the harvest before them? It always makes me wonder about the investment that God placed in front of me if I have managed to collect it well for His glory. Lift up your eyes, for the harvest is plentiful, but the laborers are few.

Read, Pray, Reflect

*"The Lord will indeed give what is good,
and our land will yield its harvest."*

PSALMS 85:12 NIV

Has your life produced the harvest you are satisfied with?

Have you properly planned and taken the necessary
actions that you should expect The Lord to
bless you with a harvest to come?

_____

_____

_____

_____

_____

_____

_____

_____

_____

_____

_____

_____

_____

_____

_____

_____

_____

_____

_____

_____

_____

Time for Sowing

Every day, we walk around, and we speak from our stream of consciousness. Most people don't realize their words go out before them as planters seeding a harvest.
Our words proceed us and create a path that we envision in our hearts. It is, in fact, out of the heart where the mouth speaks, and the condition of our heart guides us. Every day, we forecast what's in our hearts, whether it be hatred, love, organization, strategy, or success. We send out the seeds of Prophecy every time we speak, like a farmer preparing for the next harvest season.

What about the sovereignty of God and the miraculous? How should we plan our path of thriving and our walk of righteousness? Should we leave it in the hands of God to do with as He wills? Or has He made His will known, and we are empowered within our lives to sow the good seeds in the efforts of righteousness? Oh, it's so easy to blame God when something doesn't happen. Perhaps we blame His sovereignty, or we only seek miracles. What if the sovereignty of God and the miraculous support a fully empowered, autonomous person who walks with the full support of Heaven? How, then, should we plan our future? Should we leave it in the hands of God, or realize that we are fully empowered to live today, and Jesus Christ gave us His spirit as confirmation of this?

It's hard to plan success when you feel like you're supposed to be diminished like John the Baptist. I imagine we all felt the same way he did when he looked up at Jesus and knew that he was to go away so that Christ could dwell and reign. But we are not John the Baptist. He represented an entirely different system tied exclusively to the Old Covenant, the law, and the prophets.

John was required to usher in Christ and end the Old Covenant. Unfortunately, even today, people offer themselves up as leaves blowing in the wind, without control over their destinies. Do you think Jesus died on the cross so that we could be aimless babies?

Perhaps we've been told all of our lives that God is in control. The last time I checked, Jesus said, "All power and authority has been given to me, and I gave it to you. Here are the keys to the kingdom. I have anointed you with power from on high, and you can access me whenever you choose to." Jesus then left and gave us His spirit. People seem to use "God is in control" as an excuse to not plant the proper seeds in their own lives. It is so much easier to blame God for the lack that we see around us even though we're fully empowered.

We can demonstrate a healthy sowing mindset to eventually reap a harvest in every area of our lives. Sowing is a very important principle in life. There are many areas where we have the opportunity to sow. I learned firsthand the benefit of sowing in a season of plenty so that you have something to yield in times when things can be different. Thankfully, when I worked for the City of Los Angeles as a civil servant with the Department of Water and Power, I was encouraged by a coworker named Iboko, who also happened to be a fellow church member. Iboko told me to take advantage of the option to have a portion of my paycheck set aside for investments.

Turns out, five years later, after some unforeseen circumstances, including a medical emergency for my wife, I had to leave my position with that job and move to another state. I was able to provide for my family with the nearly $50k dollars that had accumulated from my sowing when it was time to do so. Imagine if I had decided not to sow when the opportunity presented itself. I would have missed out on a potential harvest that was available to me. That God made available to me. Every spiritual element or nature of God requires a physical response in order to manifest it. That's why we partner with God and speak out and declare the things that we intend to see over our lives.

It is a chance to sow in the hope of something great and wait, but we must. We must because God is faithful and true. The Apostle Paul invited everyone to follow him if they had not yet found their leader. In this principle, we follow the righteous men and women before us, and we hold near and dear to the statutes and the Commandments that the Lord has presented to us in order to walk out righteousness for righteousness's sake. We might not comprehend how our spiritual lives impact our physical lives, but we know they do, and sowing in every area of our lives is a way for us to do that.

The beauty and intentionality that come with sowing are the forward-thinking investments into our next moment. Perhaps we are sowing seeds of relationship and love. In the most beautiful ways, I think this is how the world works. Giving and sowing provide a spiritual currency that not only changes the environment that we live in but also prophesies into it. This changes the outcome because the testimony of Jesus is the spirit of Prophecy. If we are tapped into the nature of God, then we are walking out what God has for us. This is possible because we participate with Heaven and sow as the first act in our hearts and lives. Perhaps the outcomes we intend to see will be first established by the works of our hearts and hands. If you want to participate in what tomorrow brings, there's always time to sow.

Read, Pray, Reflect

"And sow the fields, and plant vineyards,
Which may yield fruits of increase."

Psalms 85:12 NIV

Are you aware that you are sowing seeds that will ultimately produce the fruit you will live by?

Do you like the type of sewing you've been doing and what it's produced in your life?

_____

_____

_____

_____

_____

_____

_____

_____

_____

_____

_____

_____

_____

_____

_____

_____

_____

_____

_____

_____

Time to Embrace

Touch is a form of manifesting an emotional feeling. The way that it engages our brain like fireworks and sends off dopamine receptors that actually physically alter our body is fascinating. An embrace is far beyond a moment of touch. An embrace reaches into the depths of our known world to demonstrate love; it coats us, surrounds us, and blankets our loved ones. It reminds me of the time when the Holy Spirit hovered over the waters at creation. The warm embrace heals the soul from the inside out because it's all-knowing, all-assuming, and all-powerful. This is why God demonstrates His love through continuous embrace throughout scripture.

It's no wonder that Christ decided to utilize touch and embrace to transfer His spirit and love to others. It's one of the ways that we're made to thrive. Perhaps, without it, we are missing a vital piece of our humanity. I remember the stories of babies born without physical affection and touch who didn't make it too long. The babies who were placed with other children and embraced had a significantly increased likelihood of survival. I don't know anyone who denies the positive effects of embracing the right situation in the right circumstances.

One of the greatest forms of endearment, invitation, and intimacy is through the embrace. Every time you meet someone, you get close, shake their hand, and give them a hug. This physical manifestation sends happy emotions through our veins. This is why it has been going on for centuries. Marriage has taught me that when it's time to embrace and capitalize on it, you can unlock doors to a person's heart like no other expression can accomplish. Life is going to present times when you are to embrace things like opportunities, responsibilities, and duty. Still, you will often be presented with a time to embrace people by embracing compassion and empathy.

Perhaps the healing of the soul starts with an embrace. And the lack of embrace could be a testament to the ability to heal. Some go numb over time because they've grown distant, and their heart is going cold because they have no embrace. I heard a rule a long time ago that I like to live by. Give your spouse at least five non-sexual embraces every day. What does this do? I believe it establishes a connection without words. It removes performance from the definition of love. It releases dopamine and continues the healing process within the body. It speaks volumes and declares to your partner that they're known, loved, and seen. What more can someone ask for?

Oh, you've convinced yourself that you are not the touchy-feely type. I understand that embrace is a learned experience, and we're all not born with it. The level of emotional awareness and the ability to open up determines the level of embrace we're open to receiving. This is obviously a correlation to what we are willing to give. Sometimes, people give an embrace in the hope that someone will return the favor. If you need an embrace, ask for it. People can't read minds. If you do not like to give an embrace, ask yourself why. Is it that you've distanced yourself from your emotional awareness and your emotional needs because you feel a little numb inside? Our scars and numbness often keep us from the things that we ultimately need.

Ask yourself why you do not desire embrace. Is it because

you're still processing your past traumas, and you don't want to get hurt again? You worry that if you let someone in close again, then you'll be hurt again, and therefore, it's easier for you to shut down and turn off your emotions. Perhaps you're someone who was trained that the understanding of emotions and the embrace of emotions is not for you, but it's for the opposite sex. So, you turned off your ability to love, desire, and need because you can handle life without it. Two things are bound to happen: emotional dehydration that leads to burnout and an explosion or a breaking point of no return.

We only manifest things that we carry inside, so if you're not a hugger, you probably don't feel very physically loved. We project the images of love, affection, and care we see for ourselves. This is the world that we live in. It's broadcast around us in microforms of our actionable demonstrations of love. If we can get to a healthy place in our hearts and minds, we will be an extension of health in all that we do as we begin to embrace the ideas, emotions, and worlds of others around us.

A beautiful thing about embrace is that it speaks a different language than words can. The physical embrace talks to our soul when sometimes words end up in our heads and never get to our hearts. This is the magnificence of Heaven demonstrated through a multifaceted love that we get to participate in. How can you deny your senses and turn them off because you've had a bad experience? Did not Christ bear the worst experience on our behalf? Should He be without emotion, without affection, without touch? No, The Embrace now has more validity because it endured pain and suffering.

Regardless of why we feel distance, pain, and suffering, we have a remedy, and it's in the embrace. The embrace that we first give and, of course, the embrace that we receive. Lord, help us know when to embrace ourselves, embrace you, and embrace those around us. Help us to know how to embrace thoughts, emotions, and actions throughout the rest of our lives. We want to know how you embrace the world around you and how you continuously embrace us so that we're trained to understand why you've given us this beautiful tool. We subject ourselves to your warm embrace.

Read, Pray, Reflect

"Faithful love and truth will join together;
righteousness and peace will embrace."

PSALMS 85:10 CSB

What is God wanting you to embrace
that you find difficult?

Are there people that need
more of an embrace from you?

Time to
Refrain from
Embracing

It's wisdom to know what to do and understanding to know how to do it. Just as there is a time to embrace, there's also a time to refrain. Sometimes, it's dishonoring, cautionary, unprofessional, unsafe, unhelpful, or unwise, but only wisdom will tell us when it's okay.

While being enlisted to minister a funeral service of a young gang member who had been shot to death, I had to stand watch and be on guard for the lead pastor and the family members who were in attendance. I saw familiar faces that were sobbing and hurting. I felt the compassion in me wanting to extend itself to embrace, hug, and pray for them, but that wasn't the time for it. Many of them I did have the opportunity to console after the services, but while I was on duty ministering, that was the time when I had to refrain from embracing, as it would have been a distraction and could have compromised the safety of those I was commissioned to watch over.

The same goes for those in emergency services. Would you prefer the EMT or ER doctor stop to give you a warm embrace before saving your life? Perhaps it's not professional and would cost you your life if time were essential. Of course, through their compassion and their love, they would want to embrace you in your moment of need, but maybe it's not the right thing to do at the time. Maybe it's better to refrain. And this is when wisdom steps in and helps us know when it's okay or not.

Have you ever witnessed a wedding in person? You're so excited for the bride and groom that you want to share that excitement with them, but you can't because they're in the middle of the ceremony. Sure, you could get out of your seat, run up to the front, and talk with the bride and groom about how excited you are for them. That would probably be unwise. "Now is not the time" is probably the response that she would be given. At least at this point in society, that's not customary, and it would be discouraged because it's not about you at that moment. It's about them, and it's their time. Perhaps you could embrace them sometime in the near future and tell them how excited you are for them. Let wisdom help you in those moments to know when not to run up to the front during the wedding to embrace the couple getting married.

Part of the refrain is learning the emotional tension within ourselves so that it serves us to be healthier individuals. Those who can demonstrate self-control and provide the world with a more refined version of themselves have learned the most important skills. To think that Christ waited thirty years before He demonstrated miracles is the most fantastic form of self-control ever demonstrated in the world. This gives us a cornerstone for our own world to have a want and need but utilize restraint. Not only are we demonstrating that we have become masters over our own emotions and that we are leading, but also that the urges of our day and the urges of our heart don't overtake us.

It communicates our ability to self-regulate and plan, and it also demonstrates our ability to be open-minded and display critical thinking skills because if we were so self-induced, then we would probably only do whatever we think and feel. Still, if we're open-minded, we will be accepting and awarding other thoughts and feelings. This will put us in a really good place down the road because we prioritize the thoughts and feelings of others, which elevates our emotional intelligence. How much wisdom shall we gain with the utilization of this self-control and open-mindedness? Surely, this is how Jesus grew in favor with God and with man. Was He the most self-aware individual that walked the earth, perhaps?

Of course, there will always be tension when we want to do something and we're not able to or can't at that moment. Maybe we're sacrificing little bits of our flesh that pull us in the direction of anxiousness, instability, and anxiety. Perhaps every time we deploy delayed gratification and don't always pursue the things that are sweet to the taste, we are becoming more like Him. It always makes me wonder what kind of process Jesus endured when He spent forty days and forty nights in the wilderness. Of course, He was tempted by everything, which would have been royally exhausting, but He proved to himself that He had power over His emotions, thoughts, and feelings. I hope that we can become more like Him in having so much self-control that we can refrain from embracing others when necessary and deploy fortitude and strength through His wisdom so that we can represent Him exactly as we should. There is no good or bad within ourselves but wisdom and knowing what to do and what not to do.

The desire should guide us, but we should not let it overtake us. We should seek truth but not let it distort us. We should be open to love but be willing to refrain from embracing it when necessary. This is magnifying the wisdom that God has set before us. His love is demonstrated in a multifaceted way, and we need to be aware that sometimes God calls us to demonstrate His love in different ways. Wisdom will tell us what we need to know if we're open to listening. And wisdom is not a historical barometer; it's a person, and His name is Jesus. So, let the time that you find yourself be the right time. Feel the pause within yourself to know what to do and when to do it. Your conscience and the Holy Spirit will guide you if you listen.

Read, Pray, Reflect

"Refrain from anger and turn from wrath;
do not fret—it leads only to evil."

PSALMS 37:8 NIV

Are you working on mastery for the Master?

If so there are things that you will have to
refrain from embracing, have you identified them?

_____

_____

_____

_____

_____

_____

_____

_____

_____

_____

_____

_____

_____

_____

_____

_____

_____

_____

_____

_____

Time to Keep

Imagine God's decisions at the beginning of time, knowing that mankind would betray Him and turn on Him, but He still made them anyway. He saw more in us than we saw in Him. Those moments must have been very difficult, having to process the sacrifice His son was about to make for the sake of humanity. The joy set before Him, which is us, was great enough to keep the plan in place. He chose to keep us, perhaps because of what we could do for Him, but most importantly, because of the joy He receives from having us around.

It's quite sobering to consider God contemplating keeping us and how that decision affects everything else. We don't exist without that choice. And given the fact that we choose to keep in the same regard that the Father chose to keep us, it brings the same sobriety to our contemplations. We may see simple decisions through our lens of convenience or perceived abilities, but perhaps some decisions have more eternal consequences than others. For example, choosing life over death when it comes to your family.

My wife had reason to believe she was pregnant just six months after we got married. She's pretty in tune with her body, as most women typically are. She took a pregnancy test, and sure enough, it came back positive. She wanted to get a checkup at a medical clinic to ensure everything was okay. The joy of having a medical professional verify that we could be sure to expect our first child suddenly turned to confusion when the same medical professional asked my wife, "Would you like to keep it or get rid of it?:

What did she mean to "get rid of it" like we were talking about an old T-shirt we grew out of? This was especially triggering to me, given that my mother told me once that my "first name was almost Number 3" because she had two abortions prior to her pregnancy with me. It's safe to say that this was definitely a time to keep, and we now not only have a beautiful daughter named Asa as a result of that decision but would go on to have two more opportunities to make the same decision in keeping the next two pregnancies alive, from which we got our baby boys, Parker and Bishop.

Is God in our decision-making process? Surely, He must be at least sometimes. To think the people of old in the Old Testament existed because of someone's choice, yet God used their life and told a story that could only be told through their eyes. It was almost as if they were predestined to live out that role for us. I believe this is the case. Fast forward to our lives, where we choose what to keep and what to throw away. A decision that could be applied to a piece of trash or a decision that could be applied to someone's life. That was always the decision that was presented before us. We have the power of life and death, and we get to choose which one we participate in.

Of course, there are always exceptions to every rule, and there are plenty of emotions to spike those exceptions. Aren't you glad that you were kept, though? So, you could debate whether or not someone else should receive the same favor you did. Moreover, so you could choose life or death and feel good about it even though the decision was made for you. God initially proposed governance at the very beginning of time. We would see this governance throughout our bodies, the people around us, and the world that belongs to us.

The governance that we have been offered is filled with responsibility where we are participating like Adam, and we are making choices. Adam named the animals and participated with God by giving them very natural names. That's what naming the animals meant. Imagine his connection to his creation as he participated with God in this endeavor. God and Adam wielded tremendous responsibility by knowing what to keep.

Keeping something is a reflection of yourself. In life, we see orders that keep trash in their houses. I imagine most of these people don't think very highly of themselves if you get underneath their psyche. If you choose to throw something away, you've deemed it unworthy of your presence and something that's not valuable enough to hang on to. Possessions are one thing, but when we choose not to keep people, it's an entirely different discussion. There's something inside of us, regardless of the label that we use or profess it to be, that tells us what we are about ready to get rid of, which is invaluable. We don't see value in it. I guess what we keep is purely a reflection of our beliefs.

As we search our hearts and assess our beliefs, our physical world will change. If we take some time and understand God's heart, then we'll know where we came from. This will help us understand how we're made and what is needed to thrive. We will keep the things that are valuable to God instead of discarding them. This will shape our world so that it's more aligned with what God has for us. It is the perfect will of God to demonstrate His will through our choice. We can choose what we keep in our lives in the macro and micro.

This is not the fault of anyone other than ourselves. It's so simple, but it has life-changing consequences. Only God knows the eternal consequences of our decisions in the moment and throughout time. May we be forever wise and follow the path that's laid before us so that we can see what we shall gather unto ourselves and what we shall discard. Lord, be our guide to never discard something that you find valuable.

Read, Pray, Reflect

*"Help me understand your instruction,
and I will keep it and follow it with all my heart."*

Psalms 119:34 CSB

Can God trust you to keep what
He wants to remain sacred with you?

Time to Give

Who can measure the currency of Heaven but God Himself? Perhaps the thing that keeps Heaven moving is the gift that keeps on giving. Jesus sustains everything, and if He is the Lamb that was slain before the foundation of the world, then everything maintains its course based on His gift to us. Can we measure the gift of God apart from what we freely receive? What eternal blessing have you enjoyed that you didn't receive as a gift? Every breath you take every morning that you get to wake up is a gift, according to God. This is how we're wired and created in His image. Eve was a gift to Adam from God to help him accomplish everything that was placed in his heart. Is this generosity flowing in our veins as a Lifeline for our love and connection?

We can surely entertain this currency of Heaven in many ways as we endeavor in our lives. The extension of oneself is not limited to physical things. We can give our emotional stability, time, presence, and thoughts; the list is endless. So much of the known world is built on the gift of the physical thing. Imagine a world built on the gift of oneself, including their Spirit, soul, and body. Is that not what we do when we get married? We exchange the former things to be a gift to another.

There are so many opportunities to give and so much variety in terms of how and what we can give, from time to money to gifts, kind words, and giving the gospel; the list is endless. We give so much of ourselves as followers of Jesus Christ, who was the ultimate giver in that He gave His life so that we may live. I went through a season while I was a young, single evangelist, giving out copies of the book The Purpose Driven Life by Rick Warren to people

I would encounter who hadn't yet chosen to believe in Jesus Christ. I remember a good friend of mine, Josh, coming to me concerned about his life in general, his relationship with his girlfriend Talia, and where they stood spiritually. After a few lengthy conversations, I was led to give him a copy of the book in the hope that it would give him some answers to questions he may not yet have thought about and could help settle his restlessness. Imagine the smile I had watching him give his life to the Lord, get married, and grow his young family to three lovely children named Peyton, Peyge, and Josh Jr. Who would've thought me giving him that book would be a small seed planted that would grow to such a beautiful blossom of blessing.

As I give my time and valuable resources, in some ways, I feel it feeds me more than maybe the person who received my gift. Psychologically, I know that giving has tremendous benefits, and it provides us with an avenue for meaning and purpose. Ironically, we don't have a tremendous purpose unless we are individuals who are generous with ourselves. Of course, God would design a world in which you have to give what you are in order for you to feel a part of the construct. The giving of oneself actually establishes oneself. It seems counterintuitive, but so is the kingdom, in theory.

What do we gain when we give? The impartation of Grace and understanding is the tip of the iceberg when it comes to our return. If the assessment is based on the investment in which our time, money, and energy are well spent, then we need to understand how generosity opens up doors that we can never open without it. I believe that there are invisible laws that rule the world based on the design of Heaven. One of those laws is generosity. Once we partake in its nature, we align ourselves with its reward. This would be a tremendous return on investment based on the Promises of God that are laid before us.

Are not the most meaningful experiences that we have in life gifts to us? Like the gift of our own life, perhaps a trip or an event of some kind. Looking well beyond the capitalistic society that we may be partaking in, we can see that giving actually keeps us engaged. Not only is it a requirement at the beginning of life that we give so freely of our time to the vulnerable and needy, but it is also a life-sustaining practice that keeps us connected with those who are around us. What do you choose to give today?

It's easy to measure a man who has nothing to give because he's empty and invisible. I'm not talking about someone who has little possessions. Possessions have nothing to do with what I'm referring to. Someone could be very wealthy and have nothing to give because they're empty and invisible. That's why the very few pennies given to Jesus by someone who had very little meant the entire world to Him. He wanted everyone in the entire world to know about her gift. Perhaps that day, she gave Him more than the material value of her offering. She must have because He wanted everyone to know about it for all eternity. Moments like these help us understand that our two cents go much further than we believe they do. We shouldn't overlook the small details of our generosity to others because it could mark our life and their life and have everlasting consequences.

Assess within yourself how freely you give and to what extent. This assessment should be practical, spiritual, and material. We live in a physical world; therefore, physical things are required to sustain ourselves. Perhaps today, someone needs a meal, encouraging thoughts, or a prayer. It's up to you to give of yourself. And your generosity has nothing to do with your physical bank account. It's a partnership with God because no one can out-give God.

Read, Pray, Reflect

"Give unto the Lord the glory due to His name;
Worship the Lord in the beauty of holiness."

PSALMS 29:2 NKJV

The Lord delights in a cheerful giver, what are you able
to give in service to further the Kingdom?

_____

_____

_____

_____

_____

_____

_____

_____

_____

_____

_____

_____

_____

_____

_____

_____

_____

_____

_____

_____

_____

_____

_____

_____

Time to
Love

What is love but the giving of oneself? Is it a demonstration or consideration? If you were to ask ten people their definition of love, they would all give you a different answer. Perhaps most would camp around the idea of physical affection as a primary characteristic of love. What if love was multifaceted and it was a spiritual power that we partner with in different ways throughout our lives? Regardless of our words or physical touch, we can connect with the realm of love at any point in our lives by doing any number of activities or through our thoughts or emotions.

Love is complex, and its understanding must be from a spiritual source because it transcends all known physical realities. How could you love someone you've never met or seen based on an idea in your mind or heart? How could you be loved by someone who lives outside of time unless the ability to love is transcending? If the source of love is outside of time, then we are entertaining an everlasting love anytime we participate in it. Maybe that's why we lose track of time and we lose our minds when we're in love.

I believe there is always a time to love, but depending on which season we find ourselves in, love tends to manifest itself differently. I remember my wife being devastated by the death of her high school sweetheart. At first, I couldn't understand why she took it as hard as she did, but watching her in mourning made me quickly get over whatever I felt personally and realize she needed me to be there for her at that moment as a loving husband. That was a time to love, and my buying a huge bouquet of flowers for the service paid off, as she said to me sometime after that, "You know, what you did while I was hurting really proved to me how much you really do love me." It's times like these that have carried me to being successfully married for eleven years now.

Love doesn't require us to understand it. How could you understand something that's eternal that we get to partner with periodically? If somebody asks you for something, but you can't quite wrap your mind around it, then perhaps it's a spiritually discerning matter. That's why it's hard to put love into words: This language that we have is so elementary in describing something so magnificent and eternal. It's easy to spot someone in love because logic and reason don't always lead their choices, but they are willing to do everything or anything to demonstrate their love.

Is this a picture of Abraham bringing his son up to the mountain as a sacrifice? Of course, it is. He was walking in the very footsteps of his Father, and God wanted him to walk out the same path. Abraham knew, though, that God would provide his own sacrifice, and his actions proved his demonstration of love to the Father. He wasn't concerned about losing his son because he knew the love that he had received from the Father.

Many books on love focus on the actionable things we can do to show our love or receive it. The Bible is the greatest gift of love because it's all about Jesus. Jesus even said the ultimate commandment is hinged on the ability to love. This is probably a conversation we will have in Heaven because it's that important to God. What is a man if he has not loved? What is his worth according to God if he does not walk in love? Only God can answer this question, but He's also the only one who's asking.

Let us not confuse love with the inability to demonstrate a healthy lifestyle and boundaries. Where there is good, there is always a manipulator within. Love does not deny the ability or the power for balance. One can easily eat too much food. The way to manifest love is different for everyone, and each situation requires a different measure of love. One can say that the wheat and the tears grow together, which is love. Also, one can say that he comes with an ax ready to chop down anything that steals the nutrition away from his crop; this is also love. The burning up of the calf is Love to God because it separates us from useless and potentially harmful things.

Even though we're called to be in a time of love, let us approach the responsibility of that love so that we may demonstrate it according to the power we've been given. This will enable us to extend the supernatural force of love through our lives to help us and those around us be the most thriving humans possible and not turn us into self-centered, prideful brats. Of course, the kind of Love that God would give us carries within it the tension of the moment and the responsibility of its inheritance. If I love my wife so much that we have a child together, I'm responsible for the love that I've given her, and I will bear the consequences of my love for her. If I have no responsibility, then I have no love.

So, the greatest extension of oneself is to give out the measure of responsibility that we're willing to accept for others. How much can I carry on my shoulders the emotional construct of those around me? How much of their emotional compass should I bear? Shall I work hard enough for them to eat, sleep, and experience comfort?

Is it not love to bear the burdens of others and create pathways that did not exist before for them to walk in a thriving life? It is a time to love; in this case, God is holding the clock because He defines what love Is.

Read, Pray, Reflect

"Oh, love the Lord, all you His saints! For the Lord
preserves the faithful, And fully repays the proud person."

PSALMS 31:23 NKJV

What does love mean to you?

How do you show God that you love Him?

Time to Hate

Does hate exist in the heart of God? The world wants
to know. How could you love something and not hate
something else? The existence of Love also creates the
existence of hate because you're choosing something
over something else. If it's not in direct opposition, it's in the
value that's established by your love. See, when I choose to
love someone, if somebody takes that love away from me,
should I not care? Of course, the existence of love creates
the option to hate. Whether it's something done to you or
for you, it's still there.

How could a good God hate anything? I suppose He hates
anything that keeps Him from Love and Joy. I suppose He
hates anything that negatively impacts His children and
brings pain, death, and misery to them. It's now justifiable
for God to hate, but it's a hard concept, nevertheless.
God's immense emotion does not limit His goodness;
it expands it. So, can one walk in righteousness and in hate
simultaneously? Of course, they can, but their hate must
surely be just and birthed in righteousness, not evil.
One cannot simply eliminate their God-given emotions,
but we must wield them in the most righteous way.

Righteousness walked out through hatred is an interesting
concept; nevertheless, it's something that has actually
served me well. I realized that I would never get off of the
merry-go-round of falling into the temptations that were
contrary to the will God has for my life until I developed
a hatred toward the things I would indulge in. It was the
only way I was able to escape and break free from them.
If God detests a matter, then should I? It would serve me
well to hate the same things that God hates because,
in every season, there is a time to hate as long as it's

rooted in righteousness. God's righteousness, not self-righteousness.

For those who are grown up enough to digest God's deep and meaningful things, let them consider this matter. It's easy in Sunday School to tell your kids never to hate anything, but then you walk out with your contradictions when you're trying to defend them from a bully, and you tell them they're not allowed to hate being mistreated. We are asking them to become performers for us. Please, Johnny, act as I tell you so that you can be accepted among your social circles. This dichotomy creates a conundrum because righteousness would hate being mistreated, but Johnny has to perform and put on his happy face. I wonder if he will be able to fully express himself later on in life.

How would we possibly know what are acceptable forms of hate if we do not know the heart of God? The context within our life around humanity comes from the biblical standards we see in the Bible. If we don't study the word of God, then how can we become it? If we don't understand righteousness, how can we begin understanding hate? This isn't to manipulate our way into mistreating people. This is understanding what value is and what's worthy of protecting. Every instance of love in the Bible is easy to embrace, but analyzing hard emotions like hatred takes some time to wrap our minds around. We must give ourselves over to the Deep and complex Mysteries in the heart and in the mind of God to understand how God could develop hatred toward something.

Let us not confuse our emotions, even strong emotions,

with the flesh. The flesh is at war with God, but emotions are simply there to express how we feel. The message within the emotion, in this case hatred, is communicating something to us. Now, it's up to us to recalibrate ourselves to create hatred for the right reasons and not for the wrong ones. Also, when we do have the emotion of hatred, we are able to allow it to speak to us so that it can show us something about ourselves or our situation. If God gave us a messenger at a particular moment, and the messenger was hatred, why would we have that messenger? What would its use be? Shall we consider the messenger evil because it's an emotion that's not socially acceptable, and should we bury the messenger in the basement of our house so that nobody knows it came?

Or did God give us a messenger within our emotions to tell us what we need to know about ourselves and about our situation? Perhaps we will take the message and we will turn it into something beautiful. We can learn about our heart's condition and improve it. We can act in righteousness and vindicate what God has given us charge over. Sometimes, we put away the sword and turn our cheek before our accuser. There are also times when we allow righteousness to rise up within us, and the only proper response is to hate the vile, corrupt, mistreating actions, pain, and misery that are put upon us and others.

Fortunately and unfortunately, righteous hatred has birthed more fervent movements unto God than others. When we see that people are mistreated, we rise up and do something about it. Hatred gives birth to life because it gives life meaning and purpose. Let us allow our bodies, minds, and spirits to communicate with us.

God, give us the wisdom to know what to do with the messengers that are in our lives. Tell us when we need to modify our hearts or allow you, God, to do it. Help us know what to hate and what to do with the emotion we're experiencing because we know you're an actionable God who brings pure righteousness, and if you hate something, it's because of a very good reason. Help us to know your heart as we explore the construct of humanity.

Read, Pray, Reflect

"You who love the Lord, hate evil! He preserves the souls of His saints;
He delivers them out of the hand of the wicked."

PSALMS 97:10 NKJV

How does the thought of hating what God hates make you feel?

_____

_____

_____

_____

_____

_____

_____

_____

_____

_____

_____

_____

_____

_____

_____

_____

_____

_____

_____

_____

_____

_____

_____

Time of
Peace

The tension that filled the air after Adam and Eve introduced sin into their lives was immeasurable. Consider the level of disappointment that the Father was experiencing at that time. He just created man in His own image, and in very short order, they flat-out reject Him! God could have easily decided to eliminate them because of their backstabbing, prideful, and arrogant ways, but He did not. Instead, He sent the Prince of Peace to redeem the broken relationship. The Father knew well beforehand what would occur and planned to have peace in the long run. It was the greatest gift that He could give to us, a demonstration of what it means to be His child, following His example, to become conformed to Christ and made in His image.

The peace that passes understanding is available to anyone who wants it. It's not what you think it is, though. Most people think that peace is the absence of activity. Like, when you sit in a quiet room and don't hear anything, that's called peace. Rather, peace is when God is present. It's His presence and nature that calms the chaos in our minds and in our world. If you are experiencing peace, it's because you are experiencing an aspect of His nature. He is the Prince of Peace.

This is one of those remarkable invisible realities that we live by. When you experience peace, it transcends and permeates your core. It affects not only our minds but also our emotions and our spirit and soul. Every thought we submit under the Umbrella of the mind of Christ comes into peace and alignment. This alignment allows us to flush out the peace we have now known. Our agreement with Christ allows us to participate in His permanent state of peace.

Can aspects of our mind and life be in chaos while others are in perfect peace? Absolutely! There will always be two trees in the garden of our mind. We choose who to partner with in every aspect of who we are. In a time of struggle and in a time of pain, we can choose the path of peace. What? Haven't you considered the tremendous evil that has come upon me, and shouldn't I respond accordingly? Isn't peace always a choice, just as Christ is a choice? I would propose you inquire upon the Lord as to His adequate response. Peace is a derivative of a healthy relationship. Where there is chaos, there is instability in the heart and in the mind.

As we consider the evil before us, we also consider our enemies. On many occasions, I've had to consider my enemies, the people who desire my demise and plan my fall. I feel more often than not that there's a time for peace and the distribution of forgiveness is at hand. When Jesus walked the earth, He frequently said, "The Kingdom of Heaven is at hand." Do with that knowledge as you will. The Kingdom of Heaven is like a throttle; you can thrust it forward or pull it back. It is in our hands to distribute and partner with peace.

Partnering with peace was one of the best decisions that I ever made because it led me to become one of my best friends. In the beginning, I was at odds with this individual, and today, we are inseparable. Perhaps I had something to overcome in my life, just as they did in theirs. When I finally settled for peace, the opportunity presented itself for a more promising relationship. Finding peace in our lives is possible, and it extends to everyone around us.

Do you feel unsettled in life? Do you feel like you're without peace? I would implore you to invite Him in. Invite Him into your mind, emotions, and situations. It's impossible to find peace in the external world. The stillness always comes from inside. The peace that David experienced when he lay outside in the green pastures was from God manifested In the flesh and in nature. Remember, washing the outside of the glass doesn't clean the inside of the glass.

Are you looking for peace in your relationships? Have you first found it for yourself? Are you trying to remove the thorn in your flesh that God has placed there, or is this something coming against you that God has given you Grace for? More often than not, we are dealing with situations that God has given us sufficient Grace for, and it allows us to perfect the pearl of great price within our life. It's the agitation of the sand that creates the pearl of great price. Every motivating thing that leads us to perfect ourselves is in Him, and this Divine agitation can lead to great things.

If you're still in the storm, can you sleep in it? There may be a storm around you that looks and feels life-threatening. Is God giving you the Grace to sleep in that storm, or should you flee from it? Sometimes, the Lord permits us to take a nap and allow His peace to wash over us. Sometimes, He gives us comfort and insight into our minds and emotions. Perhaps it's a time of peace only you and God will know.

If you abide in perfect peace in Him, then what comes out of you but peace? Oh, my beloved, it is all about choice. Even those who've been through the worst possible things that mankind could commit have still found a way to accept peace in their own lives and give it out freely. Regardless, what permission do you have to carry the sins of another when God alone has paid the price for them? Do you have special permission to restrain forgiveness from another when you have already received forgiveness from God? If we are so accepting and loving to the Lord, then we will understand His ways and walk in the peace that He gives.

Read, Pray, Reflect

"I will both lie down in peace, and sleep;
For You alone, O Lord, make me dwell in safety."

Psalms 4:8 NKJV

What does peace with God look like to you?

What areas of your life would you
like to have more peace in?

Time for War

When all other efforts have ceased, and temperament restraint is no longer an option, we find ourselves at a crossroads. On one hand, we can find the path of indifference and complacency to let our situation linger. On the other hand, we can gather ourselves and prepare for a time of war. No time that we enter into should be considered lightly because they all have lasting effects, especially war.

The first phase of evaluation should be the bedrock of our consideration when entering into a time of war. Some questions of consideration should establish the need of the hour. Have all our other efforts been fruitless, and is this our only option? Negotiations and renegotiations about vital matters that are extremely important to one's livelihood have been fruitless. Have boundaries been so exhaustively violated that there's no other option? Our boundaries, including our physical body, emotions, and mind, are all worthy of fighting for. What good are we if we're unwilling to fight for the things we value?

Have the atrocities and desecrations of oneself or the things we hold dear reached a breaking point? We can wage war on the simplest things because the fight in us creates the change. The extension of war goes well beyond oneself. We have the ability to create life and death. This is part of the role that we were given. Because we've been given the power to create death and bring something to death, we should wield it with wisdom and the direction of God.

On many occasions recorded throughout scripture, God chose war because it was His best option. It may be hard for some of you to consider that a good God would choose war, but we don't understand that it is in His mind, not ours. If we were to see things from God's perspective, perhaps we would have the same view as He does. At the end of the day, it is our mind that needs changing, not His. If God permits these actions based on the right scenario with His guidance, then what shall we learn?

The most common occurrence of war that God presents is when someone comes against Him and challenges Him in ways that are eternally violating. For instance, taking the very image of God and desecrating it and violating it continuously. God most commonly went to war with the other gods that were presented in front of Him as an opposing force of His goodness. Consider this: does a good God not have standards that are worth fighting for, or should this good God roll over and let anybody manipulate Him? Of course, anything of value is worth fighting for; we all know this, but we expect God to live by a different standard than what we hold ourselves to.

We have to wage a good war every day as we are being conformed to the image of Christ. The Apostle Peter writes in one of his letters that we should look out for things that war against our souls. I once waged a warfare that wasn't spiritual but was necessary as my health was being challenged. I waged war on carbs and sugar and lost forty pounds in twenty-eight days, getting into the best shape of my life. Wage war in all the areas you need to wage war in. Permission comes from God based on the mandates before us and our conscience.

Still not persuaded? Are you worth fighting for? I hope you answered correctly; of course, you are. If you can find value within yourself, how much more can God find value in the thing that He created? The answer is unmeasurable. He would go to the ends of the earth to fight for you and go to war for you just as He has in the past, and He will do again. How many men and women are presented to us in scripture that go to war for a Cause? The number is great. We have received biblical instruction that shows us what's worth fighting for throughout scripture. We are without excuse, the Bible says, when it comes to measuring the worth that God sees within us and Himself.

Ask yourself what's immovable and unchanging that is threatening your life right now mentally, emotionally, and physically. You can be cunning and wise when you deploy strategic maneuvers to protect yourself and fight for the things that you care about. This is not only a physical act but an attitude of the heart, as I have presented to you about my own war with my diet. Many of us need to consider the time spent battling as worthwhile because it's the only way to move forward.

We wake up, and there's news of war on the horizon. Physical, real war. Perhaps it's required because it's the only way forward. Perhaps not, but only God knows. We must hear His voice when we endeavor to fight for ourselves, for a cause, for our country, and for God. God chose David with the right tools at the right time in his life to fight Goliath. Perhaps he wouldn't have been ready if he had fought Goliath sooner. Or if he had waited a little longer, it might have been too late.

If God has called you to war, He will be with you and prepare you. His sufficient Grace will equip you to take down your enemy, protect what's yours, and protect what God gave you. Sometimes, we pursue peace and we have no results, and the only thing left is to wage war against the thing that opposes us. May we be sober in our minds as we consider the ramifications of our actions. May we also be empowered to fight for the thing that God has placed value in so that we may see an everlasting change take place before our eyes. You are worth fighting for just as God has fought for you. It's time to go to war.

Read, Pray, Reflect

"Blessed be the Lord my Rock, Who trains my hands for war,
And my fingers for battle—"

Psalms 144:1 NKJV

God has called us to wage war in the spirit,
what does that look like for you?

Time to
Keep Silent

We work all of our lives to push through the noise, pain, and confusion, and we feel powerless when we're unable to find the contentment we're looking for. We search for His voice between our words and the swirl that's going on in our hearts and our minds, and we're unable to find Him. When we cannot recognize God in our day, we cannot see ourselves. This is a part of our Eternal design. If we can't see the face of the Father, how shall we proceed with our own life because we're aimless, walking about the earth without purpose?

God can sometimes be found with the words that we find, but more often than not, He's found in the stillness. He hides in contentment to be sought after as an everlasting reward. In the stillness and silence, He presents himself to be found. Why does He hide behind a veil of peace? It's because the stillness requires no effort on our part. This is the destruction of our flesh and the end of our performance. Can we do a song in the dance for God in order for Him to perform for us? No. God presents Himself and the stillness; we must remove the noise to hear Him.

We quiet our minds when they begin to race and make our bodies still as they anxiously go about the world; our emotions, spirits, and souls are continuously moving just as the earth moves. Can we overcome it? Can we embrace the silence and the stillness to find what we are looking for? This is the hardest part for those who have received the reward for their efforts. They have convinced themselves that it is by their stress that they have victory, by their sweat that they have success, and by their toil that they have peace. To a measure, we see results in these areas, but nothing compares to contentment in the silence. This is the place of a finished work. Silence is birthed in contentment, and contentment is birthed in the finished work.

He who sits in the heavens abides in His complete work. Perfection doesn't come out of busyness. It comes out of a finished work. When we begin to realize that our access to God is from a place of completeness, then we will understand why we have victory in the silence. Most considerations unto Heaven are regarding an unfinished matter in our minds. This, however, is not the case in Heaven. God extends Himself, and His promise comes with Him, yet He does not lift another finger because His work is complete. Perhaps you have not realized it yet in your life, but that doesn't mean His work is incomplete. If the matter is settled in Heaven, then the matter is settled in Heaven. It's up to you to settle it here on the Earth.

Our gate, our doorway, is through the finished work that God has positioned before us, and the only way we can access that is if we come to Him in the stillness and the silence. We lie down and prostrate ourselves before the Lord. We must resist the urge to fill the void of our perceived need with words and with anxiousness, for we will not be heard with our many words, just like those who spout off memoirs unto themselves on the street corners trying to look religious before the Lord. God hears us in silence because we put off our performance and our baggage to meet Him for the proper reason. It is no longer about the things that we need. Yes, we will always have need. However, if we realize

He's the Lord that we're actually seeking, then what need do we actually have? If our access to Him is in the stillness, is His work not already complete and available for us?

We must be still and silent at times in order to not disrupt the things that God is doing in our lives, just as the Lord silenced Joseph when Christ was about ready to be born. Joseph had authority in the matter, and his words would have changed the outcome of what Mary and Jesus did, so God decided it would be best to temporarily silence Joseph. Sometimes, the silence is a blessing from God; either He has silenced us, or He has become silent. This can and most often is the blessing from God.

A time to keep silent is also a time to listen. I worked for a while as a manager of an IHOP and asked the owner, who was very successful, if he had any pointers for me on the journey to success. He said to always keep your ears open, especially when you can pick the brains of those who are where you want to be.

The Bible tells us to be swift to hear and slow to speak. This reminded me of the times I got to sit in my late Pastor's office and just glean from the wisdom the Lord had given him over the years. When a man like that speaks, it's a critical time to keep silent. Following this method of keeping silent as much as possible while he was speaking led to me hearing him present an opportunity that would eventually lead me to become a division leader of sales with a Fortune 100 company.

How could you say that the silence from Heaven is a blessing? Perhaps the training wheels aren't required anymore for you, and God wants you to have a little responsibility and accountability without His hand holding. Perhaps His silence is a confirmation of your upgrade and your growth in a matter. Should a father trust in his son if he's been taught well? Does that trust extend itself into silence sometimes? I presume so.

Read, Pray, Reflect

"I said to myself, "I will watch what I do and not sin in what I say. I will hold my tongue when the ungodly are around me."

Psalms 39:1 NLT

Do you find it difficult to hold your tongue in times when you feel misunderstood or unheard?

Do you believe God speaks in the stillness of quiet?

Time to
Speak

The heavens and the earth were created by design out of the mouth of God. This is why our words have so much value and weight to them. We can build up and tear down with the utterance of a word because of our authority in life. God demonstrated this in the most powerful ways before the face of the earth. Adam stood next to God, named each animal, and provided the animals with their very nature. We do this today in our cocreated efforts regardless of our awareness of what's actually happening. You and I can speak the words of life or death. The vehicle God gave us to use regularly is speech, and today is a time to speak.

I've read from experts that the fear of public speaking is the greatest fear known to man. Even greater than the fear of death, believe it or not. I once shared this fear, and just the thought of it made me shudder. I was liberated from that fear when I was asked to speak to a group of young men who were in the foster care system like I once was. Seeing their reactions to hearing my testimony, watching how much they were engaged and receiving the advice I gave them was inspiring, not only for them but for me as well. A few of them approached me afterward to thank me and told me that my coming that day was the best thing that had happened to them while they were in that facility. There is definitely a time to speak, and we have to have the wisdom to know when that time comes, the courage to embrace it, and the compassion to treat it seriously.

There are many forms of speech; only some are from God. There are different styles in which we participate in delivering our speech, and that's based on the condition of our hearts. If we are about building up instead of tearing down, then it is not only the words we speak but how we speak them. This is part of our design that we get to discover. When we speak life into a matter, situation, or person, we can measure the impact of our words. Were we planting a seed, were we reaping a harvest, or were we destroying something? This is the mystery of humanity.

Jesus went about and demonstrated His ability to speak into the hearts of individuals and provide them with the best possible path forward in life and in Him. Many would call this prophecy, but to him, it was just having the most life-giving conversations imaginable. This is something that we can do as well. We can find the treasure within those around us and mine it out so that everyone can see it. Some call this speaking the words of life, others call it being kind, but demonstrating and speaking words that come from God is not only life-changing for you to receive them; it's also life-changing for anybody who hears them.

Did you not know that you are the mouthpiece of God? Of course, you were made in His image, but the words you choose to speak out of your heart establish the very reality you live in. You're a reflection of Him and, therefore, are held accountable to the standard in which you speak and what you say. Oh, you thought you were just sharing your mind and opinions without effect. Little did you know that you were prophesying your heart into existence in the very world around you. With one agitation, verbal disappointment, encouragement, or life-giving word, you create the life you are living.

God created the heavens and the earth with one word at a time coming from the overflow of His heart. This is how we create the world that we live in. It's absolutely the best way to communicate in life because it was God's primary form of communication with us, so let's use it to advance the values and the goals of our lives and of Heaven. You, too, can become an amazing communicator wielding the words of the Divine in the mundane things of life. Whether you're whispering sweet somethings to your spouse, closing a business deal, or speaking at a conference, you can speak the deep and complex mysteries of God into every moment.

We are limited by our language and the regular use of it. It is when we grab hold of the tools that lie before us that we can wield them into something masterful like the psalms. Imagine taking individual words and selecting them together to create a masterpiece like God did with the Bible. Originally, the Bible was delivered in the form of speech or orally, and that's how everyone received it. Today, we participate in the same method because it's so powerful to partner with the right words and to know what to speak, how to speak, and when to speak. God will give you the power. He will prepare for you the remembrance of Christ and all that He has done so that you may know and have the ability to share the platitudes of God and His Commandments.

Let it be a time for you to speak and for your voice to be known on the mountaintops, not hidden or silenced. God made significant investments in you, and you made investments in yourself; it's time for you to speak them forth and become what God has always envisioned you would become. Let your voice go out before you and create the path of prosperity, spirit, soul, and body. If you have words to speak, they must be spoken, for it is time to create.

Read, Pray, Reflect

"And my tongue shall speak of Your righteousness
And of Your praise all the day long."

PSALMS 35:28 NKJV

What makes it difficult to
testify of your faith out in the world?

Why haven't you helped more people come to the Lord?

_____

_____

_____

_____

_____

_____

_____

_____

_____

_____

_____

_____

_____

_____

_____

_____

_____

_____

_____

_____

_____

_____

_____

Read, Pray, Reflect

Time to
Dance

When I began attending church regularly, I remember always watching in bewilderment at the point of the service when people would begin to rise out of their seats and show forth praises in various demonstrations. They would shout, "Hallelujah!" They would run around the perimeters like running laps on a field; they would leap or jump, clap, and dance. I always just looked on as an observer, curious to know why they acted out this way. I eventually asked an elder minister what it all was about. And he told me, "When the Spirit of the Lord comes upon your heart, you will dance like David danced." I didn't know what that meant because all of this was new to me then. But something happened not too long after that.

Again, while in a church service on a Sunday evening, I remember my little brother Darren visiting, and at the conclusion of the service, he went forward to give his life to the Lord Jesus. There was something that came over me in that moment of watching him praying at the altar of the church that I couldn't explain, and I began to clap and praise God by saying, "Thank you," and I got a feeling to move in a way that I never had before. I began to twirl around and hop to a rhythm. Anyone watching would've categorized me as dancing! It was such a wonderful experience I'll never forget. I had such a joy that led to peace coming over me as I emerged from that service. There's definitely a time to dance, and when that time comes, embrace it fully, and you'll be happy you did. The Bible says all of Heaven celebrates when one sinner turns to Jesus in repentance. I couldn't think of a better time to join in the celebration and just dance than when it's happening in Heaven!

The expression of dance is the physical manifestation of worship. This is why anyone who received a miracle from God had a multifaceted effect on their spirit, soul, and body. They would leap, shout, and dance. It's another unspoken language of God. This language, however, is expressed through the physical art of dance. Good or bad dancing doesn't matter. To dance is to express one's purity of worship; who can test it and say that it wasn't good except for God alone? Of course, we have skillful, artful dance demonstrations that show excellence and majesty. We can participate in those as well. But God accepts any form of dance we give Him because His evaluation of our dance is based on the authentic nature in which we provide it.

It may feel weird to get up and express ourselves in a way that we know we're not entirely skilled at, but who are you comparing yourself to if your act is purely for the Lord? Do you not wake for Him, sleep for Him, work for Him, and dance for Him alone? We base our decisions on the convenience of others and what they might think of us and, most importantly, the convenience of ourselves and what we believe about ourselves. If we care about those who are around us, wouldn't we demonstrate pure, authentic worship of God? What do you think it meant to God when David danced and worshiped before Him? David was probably trying to access the most authentic version of himself while displaying the most elaborate physical performance that he could present to God. What a beautiful sight to see.

Because worship takes many forms, including dance, we can exalt God through our dance and receive breakthroughs in it. The movement in our body is healing naturally. The spiritual act of dancing is also healing because we are releasing ourselves from the construct of our normal display, and we are dancing with a freedom that perhaps only our spirit knows. Dance breaks through the barriers of logic and reason, and it expresses itself in the form of creativity. As you know, the Lord is very creative.

Have you ever seen the unbridled excellence of dance before the Lord? It's breathtaking because its gestures are effortless, even though they are so meaningful. I imagine this was how God danced before creation as He was putting the stars in place and the planets in alignment. If Heaven is abounding In worship and celebration, it is also about His dance. May we find time to dance even if we don't feel like it, even if our situation does not present itself to be a dance-worthy one? May we find time to dance when we're down and when we're sad. We don't dance to manipulate him, but we dance to celebrate him.

Whether you frolic with the two steps or you are able to break dance and spin on your head, it's all worship to him. The whole goal is just to posture yourself before the Lord and release your creativity in celebration of all that He has done and all that He will do for you. This is worship before the Lord. If it goes against your carnal mind, then that's a good thing. If it challenges you and breaks you free from the mold in which you hold yourself in, then let it be so. If it's something that you've never done and you have sworn off ever doing, then now is the time. Let it be that you would recognize your option to express yourself according to Heaven and that you would find your reward in the midst of worship. I pray that you are able to recognize

the revelation of Jesus Christ and that your body so desires
to express itself that you dance as an act, as a symbol,
as an expression of His grace and mighty works.
Now is the time to dance!

Read, Pray, Reflect

"You have turned for me my mourning into dancing;
You have put off my sackcloth and clothed me with gladness."

PSALMS 30:11 NKJV

When was the last time you danced and rejoiced
in a praise for the Lord?

_____

_____

_____

_____

_____

_____

_____

_____

_____

_____

_____

_____

_____

_____

_____

_____

_____

_____

_____

_____

_____

_____

_____

_____

_____

Time to Rest

Rest: the ceasing of all efforts, perhaps at the end of the day. This is how most people approach life. They work hard during the day, and they rest in the evening. However, this is the opposite of what the Lord presented in Genesis. Every day was created at night, and when it reached morning, His work was finished. What does this mean for us today? It means that we begin each day with completed work versus needing to sweat and toil. We start from a place of completion, which is demonstrated in the form of rest. He has constructed a life for us in which we've been supplied with every good thing from Heaven to complete the work that is set before us, but we must rest in order to achieve it.

How can you rest and work simultaneously? Rest is not what you think it is. You may have proposed to lay on your couch for eight hours at the end of the day, and that replenishes you. This, of course, depends on your mindset. You could sit down and worry for eight hours, have nightmares all night, and wake up exhausted in the morning. That doesn't sound like rest. Or you could rest assured that you're completing work and enjoy rejuvenation because of completion.

This is how God operates, and every time we read about Him sitting down in Scripture, it is because His work is complete. After Jesus completed the work on the cross and said it was finished, that was His one occurrence of standing up: to witness one of His disciples being martyred. All other times, He faithfully sits at the right hand of God in His completed work. What does that tell you about yourself? What is available for you if you're able to obtain rest? Does it mean that you have reached and partnered with a finished work in your life and in the life of God? Perhaps you have found contentment in His work in you, and you are finally accepting and ready to enjoy it.

Our rest starts with acceptance. Acceptance of ourselves and acceptance of God and His works. It's impossible to rest if we don't care to accept who we are because we're at war with ourselves. How can we begin to rest if we're confused about who God is or what He has done for us? This creates a tremendous amount of diligence that needs to be walked out in our lives before we're able to enter into rest. It is the vision that allows us to prosper. If we do not have a vision of who God is to us, then how can we begin to apply it to our lives?

Most people are wanderers, which is the same description of the devil just going about wandering around in their lives aimlessly. This means they're without vision and they're reactionary in all that they do because they're double-minded, and they don't know the completed work of the cross, their position in heaven, or the measurement of their salvation. They wander around aimlessly without purpose or meaning and find no rest. This is why even the devil Himself cannot find rest because rest is only found in completed work, to which he has no access.

God gave us a template for rest in the first few days of creation, as soon as he was done with His perfected work, which was seven days. He took the last day off. Now, His efforts did not exhaust Him as they do us. He was simply giving us an example of what is required for our humanity and the understanding of what completeness actually looks like. So, instead of taking a break from our toil, we can rest in our completed work. It is the manifestation of sin in our life for us to sweat and toil, but God desires that we rest in Him, and this may be a great challenge because it is the curse of sin and death for us to sweat and toil.

The act of waiting and resting is a heavenly one. This is when we cease our efforts and cease striving to accomplish things. What are you working for if you're with God in your presence among Him? What are you trying to achieve? Even in the Bible, it was presented that if you are before the Lord, then you should cease fasting because your answer is before you. Resting in His completed works is not something that we easily understand because we have not yet seen most of them, but this does not mean they're not completed. Perhaps instead of tackling everything with our efforts or our reason, we should rest and see what God does.

Naturally, God has built into our DNA the requirement of rest. It was embracing the time to rest daily that allowed me to bring my blood pressure down and get me off of the spectrum of needing medication to regulate it. Don't underestimate the power of rest, and don't miss it when its time comes. How will you know if you need to rest? Well, the easiest way is to realize that your body, mind, and emotions are screaming at you. That's when you know you need to rest. If a loving, supportive person you trust tells you that you need to rest, then you probably need to rest. Also, if you have exerted yourself mentally, emotionally, or physically enough that you need to be rejuvenated from your work, then it's probably time for you to rest.

A word of caution: if you do not heed the calls to rest built within the fabric of who you are and your community, you will eventually break. Your mind and emotions will break, or your physical body will break. None of these outcomes are desirable because they are extremely detrimental to your well-being and to your life. You must consider rest as the grace of God that sufficiently needs to restore you, just as Jesus received rejuvenation after He was tempted for forty days. Know your limits, know your God, and rest in His completed work.

Read, Pray, Reflect

"In peace I will both lie down and sleep; for thou alone,
O Lord, makest me dwell in safety."

PSALMS 4:8 RSV

What can you do to make rest a priority in your busy life?

Jesus has promised to give us rest,
have you accepted this?

_____

_____

_____

_____

_____

_____

_____

_____

_____

_____

_____

_____

_____

_____

_____

_____

_____

_____

_____

_____

_____

_____

_____

_____

It's Time

The urgency of the hour and the juxtaposition of choice is well among us. There is a time to act within all that we do, say, or think. Our actions are a reflection of our relationship with ourselves and God. Gone are the days when we react to the world around us immaturely and presumptuously. The internal clock that we've been given, its operator is Christ. He alone adjusts the hands of Grace upon our hour. The more we partner with Him in this time-sensitive endeavor, the more we may see and experience Him in this lifetime.

The pressing seasons and situations are always there. It is only through wisdom gained or wisdom received that we know what to do in the time that we live. Shall we go to battle, or is it a time for peace? Shall we sow seeds for a future harvest, or is it a time to rest? Your inner parts that are connected with God will know if you're listening. His sheep always hear His voice. He speaks in numerous ways to those who are listening. He talks to you during the day, and He also speaks to you at night. Sometimes, He uses subtle, gentle nudges as His preference, and sometimes, He uses a loud voice. Nevertheless, He's always available.

As you go to the ends of the world pursuing your destiny and finding meaning, I hope you're on time to accomplish all that He has laid before you. Your participation is vital in this experiment called life. Every moment, every breath, every exchange of the Eternal nature of God within ourselves is precious. I pray that you find the time to be present today and that you don't lose track of time. As always, and as the kingdom dictates, time is in your hands; do with it what you will.

Self-Reflections